THROUGH
THE
LENS
OF
WHITENESS

THROUGH
THE
LENS
OF
WHITENESS

CHALLENGING RACIALIZED
IMAGERY IN POP CULTURE

DIANE S. GRIMES
AND LIZ COONEY

SKINNER HOUSE BOOKS

BOSTON

www.skinnerhouse.org

Printed in the United States

Cover design by Andrea Guinn
Text design by Jeff Miller
Liz Cooney author photo by Rachel White
Diane Grimes author photo by Steve Sartori

print ISBN: 978-1-55896-908-7
eBook ISBN: 978-1-55896-909-4

6 5 4 3 2 1
27 26 25 24 23

Library of Congress Cataloging-in-Publication Data
Names: Grimes, Diane, author. | Cooney, Elizabeth S., author.
Title: Through the lens of whiteness : challenging racialized imagery in
    pop culture / Diane S. Grimes & Liz Cooney.
Description: Boston : Skinner House Books, [2023] | Includes
    bibliographical references. | Summary: "Communication professor Diane S.
    Grimes and professional development trainer Elizabeth S. Cooney aim to
    help readers recognize how the images we experience in our daily lives
    contribute to white supremacy"-- Provided by publisher.
Identifiers: LCCN 2023003007 (print) | LCCN 2023003008 (ebook) | ISBN
    9781558969087 (paperback) | ISBN 9781558969094 (ebook)
Subjects: LCSH: Mass media and race relations--United States. | Racism in
    popular culture--United States. | Minorities in mass media. | Racism in
    mass media. | White privilege (Social structure)--United States. |
    Anti-racism--United States.
Classification: LCC P94.5.M552 U635 2023 (print) | LCC P94.5.M552 (ebook)
    | DDC 302.23089/00973--dc23/eng/2023
LC record available at https://lccn.loc.gov/2023003007
LC ebook record available at https://lccn.loc.gov/2023003008

CONTENTS

Table of Figures

INTRODUCTION

When we set out to write this book in 2019, our vision was to get more white people talking, thinking, questioning, and reading about race, white privilege, and how they perceive the world because they are white. At that time, some white people—but too few—were talking openly about racism in our society. Then 2020 happened. Amidst the Covid-19 pandemic, a racial reckoning started to unfold, sparked by the murder of George Floyd. The United States has a long history of racial injustice, and the Black Lives Matter movement had been founded in 2013, but now a newer wave of involvement and activism among white people was emerging. White people marched in the streets in numbers previously unseen in BLM protests. Books about racism, white supremacy, and how to be an antiracist ally were flooding the shelves. Podcasts, documentaries, and news stories were shared on social media.

Today, three and a half years later, we are no longer seeing protests in the news every day or activists marching in the streets. We've seen a few changes to policies and laws around policing, some intended to protect police officers and others to protect activists. Through all of this, the two of us continued to write. We didn't see other writers or scholars focusing on how to interpret images—all images, not just those directly related to racial issues—in terms of whiteness, or on how they reflect and amplify racism and white supremacist culture.

Some activists maintain that white people should never attempt to educate others, even other white people, about racism. Because how can someone who benefits from white supremacy know how *not* to perpetuate it? It's like asking fish to see the water they swim in. They're surrounded by it, they don't realize they're in it, and the water allows them to survive and thrive. The same is true for us as white people in white supremacist culture. Rather, these activists argue, white people should be led by antiracist activists of color, learning from them and amplifying their work, as well as paying them for the considerable knowledge and labor they put into educating white people.

Others believe that the labor of calling in and calling out white people, having dialogue, and working to change the behavior of people with racial privilege should not and cannot rest solely on the shoulders of people of color. White people must confront racism in themselves, their communities, and their relationships. Further, some activists feel that because white people created racism and have benefited from it for centuries, it is entirely white people's responsibility to eliminate it.

Here's our opinion. We decided to write this book because we believe it is our duty as white people to help call other white people in to conversations and in-group work on issues of race and white privilege. There is, of course, the obvious dilemma that in writing a book aimed at white people we are centering whiteness and white people's education while attempting to do antiracist work. But we need to call out racism as insiders, as people whom white people will be more likely to trust or believe precisely because we are white. We want to move readers to a place where they will pay better attention to activists, writers, and scholars of color. We realize that this approach is problematic, but we believe it is worth it.

We are not here to educate you on the history of race, racism, or white supremacy in United States or "Western" culture and society. We imagine you have some awareness of it or you would not have picked up this book. We aren't here to take credit for the work that people of color have done to identify how white people can act in solidarity with them. Some of the many excellent works on these topics by people of color are listed in appendix C, "Additional Resources." We are here to amplify those voices—to link white readers to ongoing conversations about racism, white privilege, and white supremacy.

We are also here to share with you our own experiences of confronting racism in our lives and in the media we consume. We do this not to center our own stories and voices, but for three reasons.

The first is to establish some common ground with our readers. We all have to start somewhere. By sharing some of the ways we've learned to become more antiracist and work in solidarity with people of color—and some of the many mistakes we've made along the way—we illustrate that each of us is a work in progress.

Few people are talking about how images we encounter in our daily lives—both still and moving images, in the news, in entertainment, on social media, and elsewhere—contribute to white supremacy. Most of us white people interpret such images through a lens of whiteness, or with white ways of seeing (we use these terms interchangeably throughout this book). Our minds interpret the images presented to our eyes on the basis of our experiences as white people, whether or not we are aware of these experiences and their effects. Our second purpose is to help you recognize racism when it appears in these images—to change the way you see them. As white authors, we recognize that we risk perpetuating white ways of seeing even in our effort to dismantle them. Again, we think the risk is worth it.

Our third goal is, by teaching white people to see images differently, to change the way we think, act, and create, including the ways we perceive and treat people. We hope to help create more antiracist white people living and working in solidarity with people of color by helping you more fully understand the perspectives of antiracist activists of color. We hope that our readers will come to understand why their existing white ways of seeing are problematic and will develop new, more productive ways to engage with and interpret our increasingly polarized world.

As you have no doubt guessed, this book is (mostly) written for white people. As coauthors we use the collective "we" to represent both our voices and also white people as a group. This is not a universal "we." Part of white privilege is the prerogative to think of ourselves as individuals rather than as members (and representatives) of a community. Our aim is to break through that by speaking to you from a place in our society that we all, as white people, share. In other words, there are not "good white people" and "bad white people." Rather, all white people benefit from whiteness in some way or other, though those benefits will shift depending on our other identities. Although our individual life experiences vary, we benefit from white privilege, are often unaware of our shared white ways of seeing, and often, even if unintentionally, contribute to a racist, white supremacist culture.

We expect you, readers of this book, to have a certain level of both openness and knowledge so you can work with what we're offering. There may be moments when you are uncomfortable or feel defensive while reading. As white people, we are not raised to know how to handle these feelings. We want to hold each other accountable for working through them. Images, whether in entertainment, advertising, news, or other media, tend to reflect the perspective of the group with the most power. We were not taught how our biases and assumptions influence the way we create, interpret, and use images. So we understand them as uncomplicated reflections of society and ignore (or are oblivious to) the perspectives of people on the margins (we have a lot more to say about this in chapter 2). We're here to talk about how we have allowed our interpretations of them to reinforce stereotypes. We're here to consciously recognize racial stereotypes and other visual conventions in images so that we stop accepting and reproducing them.

These commitments do not necessarily leave readers of color out of this work. It would be presumptuous of us to guess how people of color view the kinds of images explored here. If you are a person of color, you may not need this book, because you may have learned much of what is presented here in your own life, family, or community, or through formal study. However, if you grew up in a very white-inflected environment, you may still find this book useful. Visual literacy isn't widely taught; few people discuss with others, and many people may even be unaware of, how they interpret images they encounter. People of color could be drawing, even unknowingly, on mainstream (in other words, white) ways of seeing. But we emphasize that we are calling in and calling out white people, not people of color, for the creation and perpetuation of white ways of seeing. If you are a person of color reading this book, please take our use of "we" not as exclusionary but simply as not directed at you.[1] Additionally, as noted by one of our reviewers, be aware that looking at the images we present could be painful for you.

When referring to individual racial groups in our writing, we identify them by their specific racial identity. However, when referring to nonwhite people or racial groups in general or collectively, we use the term *people of color*. We chose it because it is familiar to many people in the US, while recognizing that it doesn't decenter whiteness (after all, white is a color too). And racism is not actually about different skin colors in any case, but about the meanings and histories associated with each. We know that some folks prefer other terms, such as BIPOC (Black, Indigenous People of Color), BILPOC (Black, Indigenous, Latinx People of Color), and others. Our intention in using *people of color* is not to lump all racialized communities into a monolithic group; quite the opposite. In each chapter we explore how visual conventions create racist images based on specific stereotypes or assumptions about particular racial groups. At the same time, we know that white ways of seeing blur those specifics and particularities, harming people of all minoritized races, though in different ways. The term *people of color* communicates the overarching dichotomy between white people, the supposed norm, and all other racialized groups.

We use the terms *minoritized* and *marginalized* because we want to be clear that "minority" status is not a matter of numbers. (After all, people of color outnumber white people worldwide, which is why they are sometimes called "people of the global majority.") The *-ized* ending, a verbal form, points out that the dominant group has imposed a denigrated status on groups of people on the basis of their perceived race—as it also does in the word *racialized*. We hope you will question the word *minority* when you see it in other texts.

Finally, in this book we capitalize the words *Black* and *Indigenous*, but do not capitalize *white*. Capitalizing *Black* and *Indigenous* is accepted or mandated in many styles, including much of journalism and academia. However, there is not consensus on whether to capitalize *white*. We acknowledge the argument that capitalizing *white* along with the other terms indicates the socially constructed nature of race and prevents *white* from being a universal or unmarked term. Capitalizing them all treats them all equally—yet they are not equal. Capitalizing *Black* and *Indigenous* recognizes the cultural aspects of the terms, the history of the Black diasporas, and the fact that many Black people cannot use a more specific ethnic term (which would always be capitalized) because slavery stripped away knowledge of their ethnic heritage. The term *white* doesn't have any of that history. Moreover, white supremacists often capitalize it, meaning that the capitalized form can bring disturbing associations to mind. It does so for us. Honestly, we don't want to see it capitalized hundreds of times throughout this book.

Because our book deals with visual images, it is primarily directed at readers who can see them. But those who are blind or visually impaired may also benefit from it because they may make use of image descriptions in material they engage with. It would help such readers better interpret and question both image descriptions they encounter and their mental models of what is being described—not to mention better interpret whatever images they're able to see themselves, if they are not entirely blind. It may also encourage them to advocate for or choose creators of image descriptions who are more aware of these issues, since image descriptions, like images themselves, are not neutral. No matter how straightforward they may seem, they cannot help but include the assumptions of those creating them. We hope that this book will ask questions of, and help set better expectations for, people who create image descriptions.

WHO IS THIS BOOK FROM?

Before moving forward, it's important to tell you a little more about us. We come from different generations, grew up in different parts of the country, and have different professional backgrounds, but we are both middle-class, white, cisgender women.

Diane is an associate professor of communication at Syracuse University in Syracuse, New York. She began studying race forty years ago and became interested in whiteness in 1992. Since then she has studied, taught, and written about whiteness, race, and gender. Trained in critical organizational communication, she currently focuses on difference, social justice, mindfulness, and their intersections. She is interested in how problematic assumptions in everyday life are created and recreated, how we can become more aware of them, and how we can work with them in more useful ways.

Liz is a queer writer, professional development trainer, and executive coach in Des Moines, Iowa, with a master's degree in communication and rhetorical studies. A member of the Millennial generation, she has over a decade of experience in community development, communication research, and facilitation of adult learning. Her research on visual culture focuses on the white savior complex as found on social media. She facilitates workshops on self-awareness and self-knowledge, intercultural competency, leadership development, conflict resolution, change management, and inner motivation. She is a certified consultant for the Myers-Briggs Type Indicator, DiSC Personality Styles, and the Intercultural Development Inventory.

We realize that white feminism often approaches societal issues problematically, especially around race, social justice, and equity. While we both identify as feminists, we recognize that white women have a history of excluding or exploiting work by activists, artists, and writers of color of all genders. We know that white tears are dangerous. In our writing, we strive to connect, cite, and honor brilliant thinkers and critics from a variety of racial, ethnic, and philosophical backgrounds. We draw on postcolonial and transnational feminist thought, Black feminist and womanist thought, critical race and whiteness studies, queer theorists, and visual culture scholars and artists. We invite you to take note of the people who inform our work throughout each chapter and visit appendix C, "Additional Resources," for further reading.

Our focus in this book is on underlying, often hidden, racist and/or white supremacist assumptions in images. We cannot possibly cover everything there is to know. We focus primarily on the Black/white dichotomy because that is historically one of the most profound, prolific, and deeply rooted manifestations of racism in the United States. Unlearning white ways of seeing is a lifelong journey. Like all antiracist work, it is never finished. We have seen generations of traumatic, horrific acts of racism and bigotry, and our society is filled with systems and institutions that perpetuate the grossest inequities. We must commit to building new understandings that will ground the necessary work to repair past trauma, make reparations for it in the present, and prevent it in the future. The ideas and practices explored here represent one way of doing so; there are many others.

HOW SHOULD YOU USE THIS BOOK?

Typically, no one needs instructions on what to do with a book—pick it up and read it! But because this book asks you to do more than a typical book, below are some suggestions. If you are reading it as part of a group, also see appendix B, "For Reading Groups."

- Keep an open mind and reflect on yourself, not others. You can only control your own thoughts, attitudes, beliefs, and behaviors.
- Be wary of white guilt. Accept that we're constantly immersed in a racist, white supremacist culture, recognize that we have made and will continue to make mistakes, and push to educate

yourself further. Do not ask people of color to absolve you of your past.

- Continue your education rather than bragging about it or asking for affirmation. People of color most likely don't want to be assaulted by your newfound knowledge of how white supremacy shapes literally everything in our culture.

- Get a journal or dedicate a spot on your computer or phone for reflection. Use the questions within or at the end of each chapter to contemplate white ways of seeing in your everyday life.

- Realize you are doing this for a purpose: to work toward a more just world. A world with fewer images that add to or reinforce the racial trauma experienced by people of color. A world where white people's biases are not reinforced but are questioned and challenged. Systemic racism requires systemic change; the changes you undergo as an individual do not achieve this, but they may motivate you to work toward it.

- Understand that this is a lifelong process. Your work is never done. Antiracism is a journey, not a destination.

- Familiarize yourself with the terms listed in appendix A, the glossary, and explore appendix C, "Additional Resources," to further your education.

CHAPTER OVERVIEWS

The rest of this book will show you what it means to see through the lens of whiteness and how you can start to shift your perspective. In chapter 1, we introduce you to the idea of white ways of seeing with a few examples and metaphors. In chapter 2, we lay the foundation for how our position in society, across history, influences the way we perceive the world. We also introduce you to the visual conventions that contribute to white ways of seeing.

After laying out the foundation of this work, we provide in-depth examples to demonstrate various white ways of seeing and some of the visual conventions that perpetuate them. In chapter 3 we focus on conventions that stereotype Black transgender and cisgender women and girls, including exoticization, othering, dehumanization, objectification, and sexualization. Next, chapter 4 introduces the important concept of hieratic scale as we examine images that communicate differences between white men and people of color. In chapter 5, the focus shifts to well-meaning white people, especially international volunteers who set out to help others, and how they nonetheless produce images that reproduce white ways of seeing.

The examples we offer illustrate only a fraction of the contexts in which you might notice white ways of seeing. So chapter 6 concludes by discussing how to continue working to broaden your view. We describe how to deepen your awareness through mindfulness practices. We aren't here to preach religion or spirituality to you. Rather, chapter 6 gives you resources to improve your awareness of the images you see each day and your responses to them.

White people, this book presents work for all of us to do. That work is difficult and uncomfortable. But it's necessary for the larger goal of working toward meaningful racial justice, and it may be helpful for individual self-development. We hope that you will learn to recognize white ways of seeing, and that that recognition will lead you to change your perspective and your behavior, all for the sake of a more just society. Thank you for being willing to go on this journey.

—Diane and Liz

ONE

BEGINNING TO IDENTIFY
THE WHITE LENS

One Saturday in early October 2017, personal care brand Dove released an advertisement on Facebook for its new sulfate-free cleansers. The thirty-second-long video opens on a young Black woman smiling, facing the camera with a bottle of Dove body wash in the lower right-hand corner. She begins removing her brown t-shirt, as if getting ready to shower, and a cream-colored shirt is revealed beneath. As she pulls the brown shirt off over her head, she becomes a smiling white woman with red hair. The video caused a social media backlash. Users slammed Dove for its racial insensitivity in alluding to the long history of racist soap advertisements suggesting that Black people's skin could be "cleaned" by washing the melanin right out of it. Such messages implied that white skin is pure and Black skin is polluted (fig. 1).[2]

Dove's response to the outcry was a brief statement released on Twitter: "An image we recently posted on Facebook missed the mark in representing women of color thoughtfully. We deeply regret the offense it caused."[3] Media outlets and social media users alike continued to challenge Dove, asking what mark it had been aiming for in the first place. By Monday, the hashtag #BoycottDove was trending online and Dove removed the ad, releasing a longer statement claiming, "The

Figure 1

short video was intended to convey that Dove body wash is for every woman and be a celebration of diversity, but we got it wrong."[4]

Dove is a company that prides itself on embracing and promoting natural beauty in women. That it could release this ad illustrates how white ways of seeing dominate our society. While we can't know who wrote, produced, created, reviewed, and published it, we can argue that white ways of seeing prevented Dove from noticing the racist message within it. What exactly are white ways of seeing? Let's try an activity. Grab a notebook or journal, one that you can dedicate to working in as you make your way through this book.

Visualize a group of exuberant college students, smiling and radiating school spirit. Perhaps they are at an athletic event, or maybe graduation. They look like friends celebrating together. Now imagine the students individually. What do they look like? Are they seated, standing, or kneeling? Do they have their arms around each other? Are they looking at the camera, at each other, or off to one side? What is in the background? Once you have a clear image in your head, write down a few notes that describe it.

The possibilities of such an image are infinite. However, what you imagined is probably similar to what might be seen in a real college advertisement, Instagram photo, or recruitment brochure. This is because the images we consume in our daily lives influence how we create and interpret new ones. Understanding our own ways of seeing can change the way we think about reality and how we act and communicate.

Think of your image again. Were the students racially or ethnically diverse? Was there a mix of gender expressions or identities: masculine, feminine, genderfluid, genderqueer, transgender, or nonbinary? Did any of the students have a visible or invisible disability? Were they from a certain socioeconomic class? How was that indicated in their appearance? Were you picturing students of a private university, a state school, or a community college? Did you see yourself, your children or grandchildren, or other people you know in this picture? Who was the focal point? If any of these questions were things you did not consider while creating the image in your mind, why do you think that is? Jot down your answers to these questions.

If you were surprised by any of these questions, you are not alone. This book aims to change how you perceive reality—including how you imagine it. And if you were not surprised by them, congratulations.

You bring a level of insight that will help you as you read through the examples and critiques in this book.

Let's note that actual college marketing materials have been created without consideration of the issues raised here. In 2000, the University of Wisconsin was roundly criticized for Photoshopping a Black student into a crowd photo on the cover of an admissions brochure (fig. 2).[5] Although some (white) people may excuse such "fixes" as well-meaning, they are decisions made through the lens of whiteness. They serve the interests of the school (or other organization) being promoted, while potentially harming people of color; they hide and dismiss the issue of underrepresentation of marginalized people in both marketing materials and the actual student population. Although we might hope that marketing teams would be more conscientious these days, a similar incident occurred in 2019 when York College of Pennsylvania replaced two white students with students of color on a recruit-

Figure 2

Figure 3

ment billboard (fig. 3).[6] The university claimed it was attempting to reinforce its commitment to inclusivity, but admitted that its choice of how to do so was made in haste. It's worth noting that the added students of color were light skinned, as were the students of color already in the original photo. This reflects the pervasive influence of colorism: prejudice and discrimination against people with darker skin, independent of their racial or ethnic identity.[7] Colorism can happen both within and across groups. Even while trying to include diverse racial or ethnic populations, people who see images through a lens of whiteness overvalue lighter skin tones.

We all look through the lens of whiteness; we see in white ways. In order to begin shifting our biased perceptions, we must become conscious of the histories that shape them. Shifting the way we see involves:

- Pausing and reflecting on how we see things now—the lens we currently look through.
- Asking what other ways are there to look at this image? What other meanings might it have?
- Becoming aware of and acknowledging the harm our current perspective can cause marginalized people.

- Working to change the systemic outcomes of generations of problematic ways of seeing.
- Creating images differently going forward.

There are several elements that make up white ways of seeing, which we'll be exploring throughout the book. For instance, the Dove ad (fig. 1) attempted to embrace diversity but did not consider that there was already an alternative framework by which to interpret its image. And the university promotional materials (figs. 2–3) tried to disguise and patch over a lack of diversity.

It is important to note that we will all make mistakes, like Dove and the two universities did. The 2017 ad was not Dove's first misstep. Similar incidents occurred in 2011 and 2014, which the company largely dismissed. After the backlash in 2017, the company began attending to consumers' feedback. It launched a #ShowUs campaign, inviting women and nonbinary people to submit their own photos, creating "a collection of 10,000+ images that offer a more inclusive vision of beauty for all media & advertisers to use."[8] Crowdsourcing them in this way certainly helps to collect more positive, diverse, and inclusive images for marketing, advertising, and other purposes. But preventing missteps such as the Dove body wash ad requires including minoritized creators and designers at the table when creating new campaigns. As scholar Shereena Farrington writes,

Through intentionality, brands can begin to rebuild the trust of their Black customers. A shift in societal norms will take form once the narrative about the Black group is accurately highlighted, and more Blacks are included in advertisements which seek to represent Blacks.[9]

We can all learn from our mistakes and strive to do better.

We as white individuals, rather than organizations, might respond to our recognition of racial bias, appropriation, tokenism, stereotypes, and lack of representation by feeling guilty and looking for quick fixes, as the University of Wisconsin and York College of Pennsylvania did. But those are the last things we should do. Instead of taking hasty action or trying to fix things right away, try to change the way you see the messages and images that fill your life. Start by reflecting on your experiences, your past assumptions and ways of seeing. Continue doing so as you work through the book.

As we said in the introduction, we wrestled with the complexities and contradictions inherent in our writing about this topic as white women. But we can tell you a bit about where we come from and share our experiences of learning with you, our mistakes and our new-found understandings. We can demonstrate what the process can look like as you start your own journey, going forward to uncover your stories and create new ones.

LIZ'S STORY

At the age of twenty-two, I boarded a plane to Kigali, Rwanda, where I pledged to serve twenty-seven months in the Peace Corps as a community health volunteer. Like many young adults, I was drawn to the romanticized portrayals of international development, humanitarianism, global travel, and cross-cultural living. I had previously studied in South Africa, and I wanted to return to the continent for more service-oriented work. Over a decade later, reading through my journal entries and blog posts from that time, I see the idealism I had about the work I thought I'd be doing. I was expected to share my experience online, so that friends and family in the US could follow along on my journey, and I eagerly posted photos, reflection essays, slideshows, and general observations to my blog every couple of weeks.

My intentions may have been altruistic, but the reality was jarring. I did well in the three-month training period with other Peace Corps volunteers in Rwanda, learning the language and immersing ourselves in the culture as we lived with host families. But when I moved to the village that would be my home for the next two years, the transition was a bit rocky. I was living on my own, the only English-speaking white American in the area. The next closest Peace Corps volunteer lived an hour away. Although I was surrounded by welcoming people, my novice-level language skills meant I felt isolated. I took selfies with the kids in my neighborhood and built relationships with my coworkers at the local health center where I worked. Yet, several months into my service, I was questioning everything about what I was doing.

I had originally felt comfortable going to a local community with minimal language training and practically no technical or professional skills. But I became increasingly aware of the harmful idealism that had brought me there. What I had believed to be a selfless desire to serve became muddled with an egotistic image of who I was and who I was striving to be. While my blog posts were upbeat and often humorous, my personal journal entries depicted a very different side of the experience. My energy for "helping" others, feeling "called to serve," living in Africa, learning a new language, and changing the world slowly drained as I realized how few qualifications I possessed for being there and how my presence might be having an opposite effect from what I had originally envisioned. I didn't know the term at the time, but I was experiencing the reality of neocolonialism firsthand. Why did I think it was my responsibility—or my right—to show up in a distant land and set out to solve its people's problems? What knowledge, skills, or expertise did I, a single outsider, possess to do so? Did the community even want to pursue "Western" development goals or standards? Why did I think I had to travel across the globe to do this work when my own community in the US was facing poverty, suffering, and hunger? After nine months, I was on a plane back to the US, having fulfilled merely a third of my commitment.

This moment was a rupture for me: a rupture in what I thought I wanted to do with my life and a rupture in who I thought I was or was supposed to be. When I returned to the States, I gradually became aware that my whole self-image was shaken. I didn't have the words to describe what was happening, which made it extremely difficult to process and understand. At one point during a conversation, a friend of mine cynically described her roommate as talking and acting like a white savior. This was the first time I had heard the term *white savior*, and it became the first piece of a puzzle that I would spend years assembling, searching for words to help make sense of my ruptured state.

I realized not only some of the problems with international development but how ignorant I had been of my own white privilege. When I think back now, I question how international service became a goal for me, not just as a career but as a lifestyle, a way of being. The Peace Corps had successfully marketed itself through glossy brochures, a sleek website, and an in-person presentation filled with images of volunteers who looked just like me. The images had communicated a white savior fantasy that was appealing to me, was supported by my friends and family, and had been held in high regard in American society since John F. Kennedy launched the program in 1961. When my perspective shifted as a result of my experiences in Rwanda, the rose-colored glasses came off and I began to understand some of the many advantages I held as a white, cisgender, apparently able-bodied, college-educated, straight-passing, American woman. I started learning about white privilege, white supremacy, and our historically and systemically racist society. While I do believe acts of service and humanitarianism are vital to our global community, I now see the complexities through which we have to approach such work. In chapter 5, Diane and I share with you an analysis of how international volunteers such as I was take photographs and communicate on social media regarding volunteerism and travel.

DIANE'S STORY

In some ways I had a typical liberal white middle-class upbringing. My family may have had a book or two about Dr. Martin Luther King, Jr., but my lived experience was almost all white. I remember noticing Black people downtown or sometimes waiting for the bus. As a child, I thought maybe it was not good to be Black, and I felt sorry for people who were. In other ways, my family was unconventional: intellectual, Unitarian, nonmaterialistic, radical Yankees.

We had moved to Kentucky from points north (Rhode Island, Minnesota, Wisconsin) when I was nine. I remember thinking, "People here don't know the Civil War is over," because there were so many Confederate flags. I lived in a white suburb one block away from the park and swimming pool and two blocks from my elementary school. There were maybe two Black kids in my elementary and junior high schools (though one of my grade school friends, who was adopted, was biracial—I realized this after I grew up). I went with my parents and three younger brothers to the state capital to protest against strip mining when I was in fifth grade. In junior high, I went to an alternative "free" school. In ninth grade, I refused to say the Pledge of Allegiance, but I would still stand up during it, not wanting to get in trouble.

I spent two years of high school in Palo Alto, where my perception was that there were somewhat equal numbers of Asian, Latinx, Black, and white students (in Lexington, race was seen in terms of Black and white). I remember the Black students as hostile; they pushed in front of white students in the lunch line. I had no curiosity about those kids, where they lived or what their lives were like. I thought of Palo Alto as a rich town; I had no idea that there was a struggling East Palo Alto until I heard in 1992, when I was in graduate school, that it was the murder capital of the US that year. However, in California I did learn about the Japanese internment camps the US had established during World War II. I refused to believe in them at first, since I had never heard them mentioned back in Kentucky and they sounded pretty un-American.

Returning to Kentucky and my nominally integrated high school, where white and Black students hung out in different halls and were placed in different academic tracks, I took one multitrack course because I could just read books in it. There were some Black girls in this class, but it didn't occur to me to even try to find out if we had anything in common.

Early in college, I started spending time at a developmental day-care in a neighborhood center in the Black South End neighborhood. My mom worked there; I would walk from school, hang out with the kids, then ride home with Mom. Carver Center was busy—it had a clothing bank, elderly lunch program, reading program, and large youth program. I was scared at first, though it helped that everyone knew my mom and she was well respected. I was nineteen and had never really been around Black people. When I first got there, LH, an older guy (probably twenty-five) who was a DJ would ask me every day, "Can I go home with you?" I was nervous and didn't know what to say. Soon I realized he was just teasing and began teasing back, giving him the rundown of what we'd be doing: "Sure. We'll go to ballet class, then we'll do sociolinguistics homework. . . ." Being more relaxed and using humor allowed me to understand there was no reason to be scared.

At school I was learning that Black English is rule-governed, just like any other language, and is not slang or "broken English." I read about Black culture, Black families, and a bit about Africa. Before, I had assumed that Black people had nothing to do with me and nothing in common with me. Those assumptions were challenged from two directions: Both my coursework and my experiences encouraged me to question deficit assumptions about Black culture. I could see, for example, that the kids in the daycare were smart and creative, so there must be other reasons the neighborhood was poor.

My final project for my master's degree in cultural anthropology was a report to the university's president on prejudice reduction and diversity enhancement at the university. I was still at the daycare center, writing my paper for my linguistics class on the verbal duels and games that the kids would create. I thought I was sharing how smart and innovative the kids were in their verbal play, but I realize now that my work may have been exploitative. I kept studying, but even quite a few years into the learning curve I dismissed, in typical white girl fashion, my friend Mabel's statement that Mickey Mouse was based on blackface caricatures carried over from minstrel shows. I found out later that this is entirely true.[10]

When I was accepted at Purdue to study organizational communication, my partner, who is Black, refused to move to Indiana because it's so racist. Truthfully, I didn't know either that Indiana was especially racist or that Purdue was in Indiana! We agreed to be long-distance, since the other schools I'd applied to had not accepted me, and Purdue offered me a teaching assistantship and then a fellowship.

As soon as I arrived at Purdue and mentioned my interests, a fellow student said I should read bell hooks. I learned from hooks about the idea of interrogating whiteness and was fascinated by her work on visual culture, which changed the way I saw.[11] I sought out other work in this area and wrote about it as well, though it wasn't my main area of study.

After I finished my PhD, I was hired to teach at Syracuse University, so my partner and I moved there. At Syracuse I have continued to study, teach, and write about whiteness, race, gender, and power. I mentor, give talks, advocate, and work in the community, maintaining consciousness of race issues and whiteness. Lately I've been thinking about how social justice and mindfulness can fit together.

In this book, we start from a particular understanding of US history that assumes that racism, and therefore race, was useful in the American colonies of the 1600s as tools to differentiate enslaved Africans from indentured servants and free Christian people.[12] We assume that the wealth of America was built on the backs of enslaved African Americans and on the stolen lands of Indigenous peoples. We recognize the ongoing impact of slavery in our society, as well as that of the Reconstruction period and then Jim Crow. Black and white people in the US today have grossly different opportunities and life outcomes; the impacts of history are visible in racial disparities in wealth, income, health, housing, incarceration rates, schooling, and mother and infant mortality rates.[13] There is much more history to explore, and we think knowing and understanding this history is absolutely crucial to knowing and understanding white ways of seeing.

This book is not a lesson in racial history, but it draws on history. We focus on perceptions and understandings of images: more specifically, on how our perceptions are influenced by the images' deep and complicated, but remarkably consistent, histories. To question white ways of seeing, to begin to recognize what is problematic (and why), requires knowing our own cultural and social history. For instance, you might be uncomfortable with the Dove advertisement referenced earlier (fig. 1) because you know that our society promotes the idea that whiteness is better than Blackness. But knowing that the image of Black people being "washed white" has a long history in soap advertising helps you understand just how deeply offensive the ad is. Understanding the history and background of modern images you encounter helps you understand the perspectives of Black people and other people of color on them.

WHAT IS WHITENESS?

First, let's clarify a few things about whiteness. Whiteness is not biological; it is a cultural construct that exists only because it is continually recreated. Nonetheless, it has life-and-death consequences.

Most white people don't really think of ourselves as white in our day-to-day life. White antiracist scholar Jean Ramsey tells the story of how, having actually written an article about how white people don't see themselves as having a race, she was once talking with a Black colleague about a different study. Her colleague kept referring to four racioethnic groups in the study, while Jean continued referring to three. He patiently repeated himself, until she finally realized he was counting whites as a racioethnic group, and she was not. "There I was, caught being stupid again," she writes wryly.[14]

We must recognize that we white people have a race, are part of a group that has that race, and that this impacts our experiences as well as the experiences of those around us. Many white people think whites are the "normal," "universal," or "default" population and therefore are not raced, and that other people do have race simply by virtue of not being white. Liz admits that when she was younger, she thought that places and people in other parts of the world had interesting, unique "cultures" while the US had none. Places like Ghana, India, China, and Japan had real traditions, celebrations, food, and so forth, but America was blandly "normal." This belief is common among people raised in the US, and especially among white people.

Not only do white people have a race (which, like all races, is a social construct), we have particular experiences and advantages because of it. We're often unaware of this, tending to think of ourselves as individuals with unique histories, worldviews, and lives, indeed as individuals who've worked hard for what we have. Individualism is deeply ingrained in us. We may associate ourselves with a group identity, but it is rarely the first thing that defines us—and rarely is that group a racial one. For instance, you might think of yourself as a member of your gender, nationality, heritage culture, or religion before thinking of yourself as white. Our ability to consider ourselves primarily as individuals is a privilege given to us because of our whiteness. Throughout this book, we refer to you, dear reader, and ourselves as part of this larger group: white people. We are challenging you to shift your perspective and consider the stereotypes that may come to mind, and the restrictions and lack of control you may feel, when you are referred to as part of a larger group. Your unique experiences and background are not what matter here.

To most of us, our whiteness is usually invisible. We don't notice or think about it because we don't have to. We can live our lives, make choices, interact with others, and pursue our goals without thinking about our race. White scholar-activist Peggy McIntosh uses the metaphor of an invisible backpack in which she carries around all of the privileges she, like all white people, has, simply because she is white.[15]

For instance, she can spend the majority of her time with people of her own race, not fear being singled out by police because of her race, shop without being followed, and see people who look like her well represented every time she turns on the TV or opens a newspaper. And she admits that she had trouble remembering the many privileges she uncovered until she wrote them down. She also draws a parallel between men's obliviousness to male advantage and white people's obliviousness to white advantage. McIntosh argues that both forms of unconsciousness are firmly grounded in US culture and function to keep power in the hands of the same group of people over time. Awareness of our own whiteness is one step toward challenging that imbalance of power, and in chapter 6 we will discuss mindfulness as a way to deepen that awareness.

The study of whiteness is not new. Black, Indigenous, Asian, and Latinx scholars such as Anna Julia Cooper, Gloria Anzaldua, James Baldwin, Chrystos, W. E. B. Du Bois, Maxine Hong Kingston, Toni Morrison, and Ida B. Wells-Barnett have thought and written on it for at least three centuries. But it's becoming more widely discussed in both academic and popular circles. Although the Black Lives Matter movement was founded in 2013 by Alicia Garza, Patrisse Cullors, and Opal Tometi after the acquittal of Trayvon Martin's murderer, it was the murder of George Floyd in May 2020 that prompted many white people to try to understand our racist history and racist present for the first time. Books, podcasts, YouTube videos, and articles flooded mainstream news outlets and social media. At the same time, many politically conservative people accused critical race theory of being a poisonous lie. Attempts by school boards to ban books and history curricula that might make white parents uncomfortable, such as the 1619 Project (spearheaded by Nikole Hannah-Jones), continue to this day.

Because whiteness is often invisible to us, we never learn how to talk about race. The adults who raised us never needed to talk to us about what our lives would be like as white people, never had to warn us to behave in certain ways because our behavior would be judged in light of our race. Nor did they usually talk to us about race at all, beyond buzzwords or platitudes. We didn't have actual conversations about the deep racial divides in this country—and we still don't. They passed down to us their desire to avoid issues of race, to feel no responsibility to work toward racial justice, and this is why we love terms like *diversity, equity, inclusion, belonging, colorblind*, and *multicultural*. They allow us to seem to be progressive while not using our white privilege to create system-changing action. We can live our lives without fear, unaware of the privilege, power, and protections we have and unaware that those who are not white pay for them. Writer Layla Saad argues that "you cannot change your white skin color to stop receiving these privileges, just like BIPOC cannot change their skin color to stop receiving racism. But what you *can* do is wake up to what is really going on."[16] As Saad points out, white people are kept unaware of white supremacy because the system was designed to keep them unaware.

Therefore, as white people, we tend to respond to discussions about race and privilege with silence, with withdrawal, with recourse to theory or hypotheticals, with guilt or shame, frustration or anger, even sadness and tears. We deeply resist learning about these issues. But it is time for us to stop. We need to challenge the ways whiteness dominates our society. This is precisely the aim of this book—to, as bell hooks puts it, interrogate whiteness in the images we look at every day. To do this as white people is extremely difficult. As one of our reviewers pointed out, our underlying and subconscious beliefs of superiority leave little room for critical thinking, reflection, and accountability.[17]

However, striving to do this brings us one step closer to creating a more just and humane society.

In her book *I'm Still Here: Black Dignity in a World Made for Whiteness*, Austin Channing Brown writes,

> White people desperately want to believe that only the lonely, isolated "whites only" club members are racists. This is why the word *racist* offends "nice white people" so deeply. It challenges their self-identification as good people. Sadly, most white people are more worried about being called racist than about whether or not their actions are in fact racist or harmful.[18]

We must keep learning in spite of—or perhaps because of—our discomfort or fear. As the saying goes, we must "learn to be comfortable being uncomfortable."

WHAT ARE WHITE WAYS OF SEEING?

We are going to use a physiological metaphor to expand our understanding of the concept of white ways of seeing. White ways of seeing operate at the level of interpretation, but they're somewhat similar to the physiological phenomenon of the blind spot. The following experiment will illustrate that phenomenon; we describe its results for readers who may not be able to do it themselves.

Hold figure 4 out in front of you, with the x about twelve inches in front of your right eye. Cover or close your right eye while focusing on the x with your left eye. You should see the dot in your peripheral vision. Now slowly bring the book toward you, keeping your focus on the x. You will notice that the dot on the left disappears from your peripheral vision, and then reappears as you bring the book still closer.

Figure 4

Pause with the book at a distance where the dot disappears. This is your blind spot.

Now switch sides. Close your left eye while focusing on the dot with your right eye, and once again bring the book slowly closer until the x disappears and then reappears.

What's actually happening here? When light hits the retina of our eye, small cells called photoreceptors register it and send signals through the optic nerve to our brain, which assembles the signals into a picture. However, there are no photoreceptors where the optic nerve attaches to the retina. Light that hits that spot thus can't be registered; we can't see anything with it. This is our blind spot.

We don't usually notice our blind spot because for those with two eyes, each fills in what the other can't see. Our brain combines the partial images from each eye into a full picture, filling in whatever seems to be missing. To see this in action, draw a line straight across the figure, right through both the dot and the x to both edges of the page (or grab a piece of paper and draw your own version). Try the experiment again and pause again where the dot disappears. You will find that the line seems unbroken.

This physiological phenomenon is a metaphor for the ways we interpret images. Of course, white ways of seeing are not based in physical reality, like the blind spot of our eye. They are socially constructed. But just as when light from an object strikes the blind spot of our retina, we may think we are seeing the whole picture when in reality we are missing part of it. And just as the brain tries to guess what's

19

missing, showing us an unbroken line that does not truly exist, we may bring inaccurate ideas and meanings to our interpretations of what we see. In both cases, what we *don't* see creates a way of seeing. Unless someone shows us this gap in our reality, we go on believing we are seeing things as they truly are.

We have blind spots, literal ones because of our anatomy and metaphorical ones because of our white ways of seeing. And while they are not our fault, once we have become aware of them we are responsible for constantly checking for what we may be missing, misunderstanding, or misinterpreting in the images we see every day.

Author and spiritual teacher Andrew Holecek notes, "Buddhists have long observed that we don't see things the way *they* are; we see things the way *we* are. The 8th-century tantric master Padmasambhava said, 'Changes in one's train of thoughts produce corresponding changes in one's conception of the external world. As a thing is viewed, so it appears.'"[19] Throughout this book, we teach you to be aware of what happens when we see images primarily through the lens of whiteness. Here are some examples to start off with.

- We see ourselves always represented without awareness that this is a privilege.
- We fail to see the connection between historical racism and racist symbolism in modern images.
- We fail to recognize why certain pictures are harmful or inappropriate to post on social media.
- We don't understand how the camera angle, framing, and spatial relationships within an image can convey meaning, including racism.
- We don't understand the difference between cultural appropriation and cultural appreciation in the images we see or create.

- We fail to notice when other races are underrepresented in images.
- When we do see other races represented, we believe that representation is enough, without attending to or understanding issues of appropriation, tokenism, and stereotype.

Take a moment to think about the number of images, both still and moving, you encounter each day. We are surrounded by photographs, illustrations, cartoons, emojis, videos, and graphs; we encounter them in advertisements, on YouTube, on TikTok, in magazines, on social media, on websites, and in innumerable other contexts. And when we look closely at them, we begin to notice how often stereotyping and racial bias appear, how often whiteness is centered. We start making connections between historical contexts and today's images, understanding how our social conditioning influences our perspective.

We can't do this work alone. What may be obvious to someone else may be invisible to you. Understanding the ways we see requires admitting that our perspective is not the only one. Everyone can realize that there will always be things outside their own perspective. But because white people have more power in society than people of color, our perspective can cause more problems if it is unexamined. Our blind spots may change or evolve, they may get smaller over time, but they will always exist. The risk is of being unaware that they exist at all.

Even when we recognize our blind spots, we do so through a white perspective. Being white means we will continue to see everything—including images, ourselves, and others—through the white lens of our life experiences, position in society, and knowledge and understandings. One of our readers described white ways of seeing as looking through a veil.[20] Our goal with this book is to give you the tools to become more aware of your own white ways of seeing.

You may be thinking one or more of three things right now—common reactions among white people who are challenged to come to this awareness.

You may be thinking, "How can you say this about *me*—all white people's ways of seeing are not the same! What about a white person who grows up poor, living in a neighborhood that is mostly people of color? They're not in a white bubble; they interact with people of other races every day. They will have a very different experience of whiteness and race!" And that is true, as far as it goes. But all white people are offered images that center whiteness and stereotype people of color. These images can do this so strongly that they shape white people's interpretations more than their actual experiences with people of different races do. White people are very likely to be unaware of this happening, and we will discuss in chapter 2 some of the reasons why.

And you may be thinking, "How can you say this about *me*—you don't know me!" We're arguing that yes, we do know you—us—as white people. We have commonalities as white people, even if we're not aware of them, and even if we don't think of ourselves as having a race, as being "white people." As scholar Charles Yancy puts it, we maintain the illusion that we are individuals and that our accomplishments and achievements are due solely to merit.[21] At the same time, we think of people of color as members of their racial group. The tension between seeing ourselves as individuals but people of color as part of a group is often invisible to us, and it has serious implications. For example, it conceals the accumulation of white wealth over generations, denies how dominant groups shape our culture and socialization, perpetuates the myths of meritocracy and colorblindness, and ignores systemic racism.

We understand that by addressing white people as a group through-out this book, we are doing to you what we say to stop doing to people of color. Our intention is not to be hypocritical. For white people, the experience of being generalized about, stereotyped, and treated as a group can contribute to unlearning white ways of seeing. It may remind us to not do the same to others. Moreover, it was other people—our group, our culture, our society—that taught us to see ourselves as independent, separate individuals in the first place. We hope the irony is not lost on you.

Lastly, you may be thinking, "How can you say this about *me*—I'm 'woke'! I'm doing or have done the work to see what is in my blind spot!" Remember, the veil that we look through has many layers. We assume that you have begun working on understanding your own white privilege, so you have unpeeled some layers already. But are you really going to tell us you have no blind spot, when the definition of a blind spot is that you can't see it? If you feel defensive, just notice the feeling. Welcome to the place you may be in often while reading this book: outside your comfort zone.

As white people, we can be kind, openhearted, and generous, and, simultaneously, harmful to people of color. Tools like the Harvard Implicit Association Test reveal that most white people unconsciously prefer other white people to people of color.[22] Although ways of seeing do vary, white people may be more likely to assume that ours is correct if it reflects back to us our learning and experiences. Our goal is to help you see how whiteness underpins your interpretation of images. The tools and examples in this book work against your early learning and society's training of you to be a "good white person."

QUESTIONS TO CONSIDER

- How do you define whiteness?

- Are you aware of any of your blind spots already? What are they?

- How has your race impacted the way you experience and perceive the world?

- What emotions come up for you when you recognize this impact?

- What does it feel like to be grouped, labeled, and spoken to as one instance of a category?

TWO

THROUGH THE LOOKING-GLASS

Reality, Culture, and the White Lens

On a recent trip to Wisconsin, Liz was walking with some friends along a path in the lake town where they were staying. As they admired the marina, a middle-aged white woman who was part of Liz's group noticed a statue of a Potawatomi chief and hopped up to pose with it, jokingly putting her arm around the figure and pretending to kiss him. Another white person in the group stopped and, laughing and playing along, took a photo of the woman posing. People often pose and joke with statues in this way, especially when visiting a new place. However, this particular instance is offensive because of the racial dynamics at play. This white woman didn't see the statue as representing the sacredness of the ground on which she stood, which had been transformed into a marina and a vacation spot for tourists. Her posing and mock kiss demonstrated that she felt entitled to act as she wished in that place.

You may not think this is an example of racism and white ways of seeing. Perhaps you are thinking there was no harm done to a real person, and that she wouldn't have done such a thing with an actual Potawatomi chief. But this kiss, however innocent and fun it may seem, occurred in a context in which men of color are often presented as backdrops, decorative and dehumanized. One example is a fashion ad in which an Asian woman has her arm around a Black man's head, her hands covering half his face, pressing her cheek to his, pulling him off-balance. He looks down, head slightly tilted away from her. He has lipstick on his cheek while she looks at the camera aggressively, with her lips puckered for another kiss. The author's caption for the image notes: "A man of the black eunuch type handled, fondled as a toy."[23] Such images are everywhere, and they are harmful whether or not they were intended to be. Liz tried to call in the two women for their offensively racist actions, but they minimized them and criticized Liz for being too serious when they were just trying to have fun.

At another time on the same trip, Liz was staying at a resort with her family, where she read a display describing the land the hotel sat on as a "once-sacred" burial ground for the Potawatomi tribe. The text described how the "imposing burial mounds" had been removed, the various artifacts that were "uncovered" during excavations, and how the lake's Potawatomi name had been replaced with an English word. And it went on to introduce the white European man who "discovered" the lake.

The phrasing of the display and the incident with the statue are examples of how white people inappropriately see spaces and monuments as ours to use and change however we please. We then commemorate this perspective through documents, plaques, names, before and after images, and narratives, which in turn permit or even encourage disrespectful behavior like pretending to kiss the chief. Further, we often don't see the racist perspective, language, appropriation, and use of stereotypes in these moments. When confronted, we may minimize, dismiss, or justify our actions, calling them "just a joke," "not a big deal," or not racist at all.

If we strive to be antiracist, fight for social justice, and help make the world a better place, we must first of all reflect on and critique ourselves. In this chapter, we challenge and complicate the reality that you think you know, the one we, as white people, have built our lives around. We are talking about our perceptions, and about how we communicate (or fail to communicate) about them. And we start with a big question.

WHAT IS REALITY?

Try this exercise. Look at a tree: out your window, on your phone or computer, or even in your imagination. What do you see? How do you describe the tree? What purpose or meaning does a tree hold for you? Write down your thoughts.

Now think about what a tree might look like, and what it might mean or symbolize, to someone else. For instance, what could a tree mean to a lumber company executive, an artist, or an environmentalist? Would it literally look different to each? Perhaps the executive would see a lucrative (or not!) species, with a large, straight trunk. The artist might see the shape of the tree's branches, its unique colors and shadings, how the light plays on it, and how it fits into the landscape. Maybe the environmentalist would see it as part of the ecosystem helping to protect the planet, or as in need of protection itself. Each person in this example is looking at the same tree. However, because they have different perspectives—different assumptions, backgrounds, experiences, skills, educations, and goals—they are seeing it and understanding its meaning or purpose in dramatically different ways.[24]

This exercise is a simple example of an important point: that the way we understand, see, and make meaning of reality depends on our particular culture, experiences, education, language, and upbringing. Our assumptions, our experiences, what we've been taught, and what we've unconsciously absorbed shape how we understand what we see, and even what we take to be reality. In this book we argue that *reality is socially constructed through communication.*[25]

That's a big claim, but it's really important—it underpins everything we talk about here. In this section we work backward through the phrase *social construction of reality*, explaining each significant word in turn.

SOCIAL CONSTRUCTION OF *REALITY*

First, what do we mean when we use the word *reality*? We're born into a reality, and we accept it as, well, real. We don't naturally see it as having been created by people, but it is. The meanings of things are stabilized (and sometimes changed) through conversations among many people over long periods of time. They will be different in different places, even at the same moment. When we realize this, we understand that reality can't ever be universal.

Believing the reality we're born into is the true or only reality encourages us not to question things, and not to feel responsible for any aspects of our culture we find problematic. On the contrary, failing to realize that we continually recreate our cultural meanings makes it easy for us to blame them on others. Enmeshed or ensnared in what we take for granted, we pass it on to our descendants. Although this certainty can reduce our anxiety and give structure, stability, and meaning to our lives, it is false, based on naiveté. It leaves us stuck with something that is both unchanging and problematic.

And we're usually unaware of all of this. Let's take an example. If you were raised attending public school in the United States years ago, you most likely went to a classroom whose form hadn't changed much since schooling systems were formalized in our society. Historically, school classrooms had desks bolted to the floor in rows, facing a chalkboard, in front of which the teacher stood instructing you. If this is the picture in your mind, you may accept this as the reality of school. The teacher is in the front because they're the one who has knowledge and authority. The students sit at desks because they have no authority and are there to gain knowledge. The chalkboard is there for the teacher to write things on that the students should memorize and thereby "learn." In this traditional classroom, there are no other formats in which to learn—sitting in a circle, in small groups, in pairs, moving around, collaborating in creating something—otherwise the desks would move. Nor are the students meant to learn from each other. The bolted-down desks convey that sitting still and taking notes is the way to learn. This classroom encourages us to assume that this is the best way for students to learn and for teachers to teach, and that school has always been and will, or should, always be this way. If issues arise in this setting, such as kids misbehaving, the adults do not need to take responsibility for them. They assume there is something wrong with the kids themselves, not with the space itself or the process of teaching in it. And they do not even realize that they are making these assumptions, let alone question them.

This book is partly concerned with becoming aware of our personal assumptions, and in our last chapter we discuss some tools to build this awareness. But there are broader cultural and societal assumptions that likewise need to be questioned, analyzed, and reflected on. We accept the culture and reality that we are born into, such as the way classrooms are designed and what their design implies about the proper nature of education. And when our personal experiences are reflected back to us in the broader cultural experience—for instance, when we see other schools full of similar classrooms—our belief that this reality is true and right is strengthened. In a cycle of reinforcement, our assumptions lead us to create physical structures and belief systems that reflect them, and the next generation accepts those structures and systems as real—"just the way things are"—and makes assumptions based on them. We take our creations for granted, forget that we created them, and then act as though they have always existed.

The cycle is only disrupted when we are exposed to a different way of doing things. Using the classroom example again, when we experience, imagine, or learn about a different school environment we can start to believe there are other ways of learning or teaching. Classroom design and structure evolved over the decades. In other words, these changes didn't happen rapidly. If we've seen new ways work, or heard or read about them working, we may be open to adopting them in our own schools: instituting peer learning, allowing unstructured time, or unbolting the desks from the floor. Today, the traditional classroom setup remains as one option among several. However, most people resist change and take a long time to accept it. The few who are open to other ways of doing things are often met with defensiveness, hesitation, and fear of the unfamiliar. Yet, once enough time has gone by and enough of us have accepted the change, it becomes the norm, the new reality, and we forget that things were not always this way.

SOCIAL *CONSTRUCTION* OF REALITY

The next word in the phrase is *construction*. On a basic level, we understand it to mean creating or building something. As we're exposed to different realities and different traditions, we start to realize that the values, rituals, and practices we take for granted were all created by humans at some point. And then we realize that, if necessary, they can be reinvented (not easily, but it is possible). In the context of the social construction of reality, *construction* refers to how we create language, pictures, and ultimately stories about things in order to make sense of them.

We create stories to help us understand who we are, where we came from, and where we are headed. However, as we have said, we each carry our assumptions with us. When we make meaning of something, it is meaningful to us because we created it. But there will be others for whom our meanings are meaningless, our stories incoherent. We must always ask who is telling a given story, and why.

Most Americans are familiar with the Horatio Alger story, in which a plucky person—traditionally a man—"pulls himself up by his own bootstraps." This myth-story tells us that individual hard work, dedication, and merit will result in a successful, rewarding life. As white people, we likely believe this myth. That's because it stems from the perspective of the group with access to power and resources that make it easier for group members to "pull themselves up" than it is for others; they are in fact doing it not by themselves, but with help. And the story fits with other cherished notions, like individualism and meritocracy.

Does this mean every white person in the United States can pull themselves up by (supposedly) their own bootstraps? No, but they are more likely to be able to than are those impacted by long-standing racial oppression, who lack opportunities, resources, education, access, or a way to communicate. As the saying goes, "You can't pull yourself up by your own bootstraps when you don't have boots!" And when marginalized groups can't succeed on the terms of the narrative constructed by the dominant group—because they face obstacles that were put in place by the dominant group—the dominant group constructs another narrative about why that is. Often that story is that marginalized people are lazy, stupid, or just unworthy.

The bootstrap story is just one of many that we in the US draw on to make sense of our history and experiences. Yet, although we believe so deeply in these stories, they are local and partial. So are our understandings and stories about race and whiteness. But even if we all have different perspectives on reality, the process of social construction through which they are created is the same. Understanding this helps us be patient with ourselves and with others, especially when they see the world very differently than we do.

SOCIAL CONSTRUCTION OF REALITY

Now, we don't sit around telling stories to just ourselves. Our families, friends, places of worship, neighborhoods, and communities influence our reality and help us create meaning in our lives. This is why the phrase begins with the word *social.* Our world may seem solid and universal, but it is the product of thousands of years of conversations and collaborations among human beings. It seems definite to us partly because most of the people around us probably make assumptions similar to our own. When we understand it as socially constructed, we are more aware that other people may have very different ways of living and thinking, ways that were created out of the stories they grew up taking for granted about reality (which they will also pass on).

Understanding our reality, and all realities, as constructed in a social context brings us into a different relationship with other cultures, other ethnic groups, and other religious traditions. Though it is almost always easier to see the cultures and traditions of others as constructed while still viewing our own as real, we nonetheless get an inkling that our way of living, our assumptions, are only one set of possibilities among many. We start to realize that other peoples' reality is just as real, comforting, and familiar to them as ours is to us.

So, if we put all these definitions back together and in the right order, what do we have? *The social construction of reality is the process of creating meanings in collaboration with others, but then taking these creations for granted, forgetting that we created them, and eventually treating them as if they always already existed.*

It's important to note that the social construction of reality is not "good" or "bad" in itself. It is just the way things are. But we need to acknowledge it.

As communication scholars we want to emphasize that saying that reality is socially constructed means that it is constructed—and sustained, and changed—through communication. In this book, we focus specifically on visual communication through images. How do these images influence our understanding of reality, and whose reality is it?

Remember, it is in the interests of those with power to try to control meaning. We don't usually realize this, because we experience reality as a given rather than as socially constructed. But when we understand it properly, we know that reality is profoundly open to our collective influence. Through the power of language, symbols, and images, we can make a difference. We can construct new ways of understanding and communicating that will encourage new possibilities. We can make problematic ways of seeing visible to ourselves and others so we can learn from our mistakes and do better in the future.

NOT ALL PERSPECTIVES ARE CREATED EQUAL

Being caught up in one socially constructed way of seeing makes other ways of seeing unavailable to us. We believe what we see, and we fail to recognize that there's a lot we don't see. In other words, as white

Figure 5

rhetorician Kenneth Burke says, a way of seeing is also a way of *not* seeing.[26] The cartoon in figure 5 illustrates this. Two people are standing facing each other, and on the ground between them is a number. One person is arguing, "It's a 6!" and the other person, standing at the number's other end, is arguing, "No, it's a 9!"[27] This is an example of dualistic thinking, which also underlies notions of us versus them, good versus evil, and Black versus white. Dualistic thinking leads those committed to one way of seeing things to reject the other.

Seeing things from only one perspective happens when we aren't conscious of the fact that reality is socially constructed and that other people may be experiencing very different realities. It then becomes difficult for us to know how someone else may perceive the world because we're so caught up in our own way. And this happens all the time in our everyday life.

Our analysis gets more complex—and more accurate and useful— when we consider differences in power. Here we draw on what is known in the field as standpoint theory.

Standpoint theory suggests that where you stand metaphorically (meaning where you are positioned in society) affects what you can see. You know that this is literally true if you've ever been to a concert and ended up in the General Admission section behind a much taller person. It impacts your entire experience, right? But it is also metaphorically true in more complex situations. For example, if the images we see in textbooks or mass media reflect our experience, our social position, we don't question them. But someone who is part of a minoritized group, whose experience and standpoint are not reflected in those images, is more likely to. If the few images they see of people who look like them reflect stereotypes or are nothing like the real people in their life, they may reject those portrayals. Such a person can see and know both the center (the mainstream perspective on both itself and "minority" groups) and their own experiences out on the margin.[28] They are less likely to assume that the images they encounter reflect reality. For example, filmmaker Chico Colvard, creator of the 2018 documentary *Black Memorabilia*, notes, "From Uncle Remus and Aunt Jemima at breakfast, to the Little Rascals, Shirley Temple and Bugs Bunny in blackface on Saturday morning TV, to Uncle Ben staring at me from the cupboard—these exaggerated and demeaning representations of African Americans were alien to the hardworking and dignified people I knew."[29] Alternatively, they may internalize the racism they encounter, or feel pressure to conform to those stereotypes.

Because white people tend to only see the center and not the margins, we think our reality is the only one. Marginalized groups may see both their own version of reality and the mainstream's. In the cartoon in figure 5, we white people are the ones arguing, maintaining that there is only one reality and the other person is wrong. But minoritized or marginalized people are the ones looking at the cartoon, able to see that both realities are incomplete and uninformed, aware that there can be multiple interpretations, understandings, and knowledges about reality.

Though standpoint theory talks about multiple margins, because people are marginalized in multiple ways (such as by gender, race, class, sexuality, ability, education, language, religion, and nationality), we also want to acknowledge the concept of intersectionality. Theorized by Professor Kimberlé Crenshaw, a legal scholar and activist, intersectionality is the recognition that each individual's identities intersect and overlap.[30] Crenshaw developed her concept by emphasizing that when a woman of color files a lawsuit for discrimination, a legal system that forces her to base her claim solely on either racial or gender discrimination can obscure the full force and impact of what she has faced, because prejudice is based on the intersection of all her identities. Intersectionality recognizes that people with multiple disprivileged identities, such as women of color, disabled queer people, and so on, have experiences and perspectives that are not just the sum of their identities considered in isolation.

Intersectionality applies to white people as well. We may be aware of biases or assumptions connected to our marginalized identities, whether they concern gender, sexuality, disability, or something else. But we often continue to miss the impact of our whiteness on our experiences. Our whiteness impacts all other aspects of our identity and our relation to power. A gay white person may be less privileged because of their sexuality, but they always retain the privilege that derives from their whiteness. And all oppression is not the same; being oppressed on a nonracial axis, such as gender, does not mean we can understand what people of color go through. In this book we do not minimize or disregard other identities, but we avoid diverting the conversation to them so we can focus primarily on the issues of whiteness.

OUR VISUAL CULTURE

We are talking about the ways we perceive reality because they affect how images are created and interpreted. Think of the thousands of forms of visual communication we encounter: photographs, billboards, websites, memes, gifs, social media posts, illustrations, graphic design, PowerPoint slides, product labels, logos, cartoons, advertisements, and TikTok videos. We may see four to ten thousand advertisements alone in a day.[31] If all of those images are based in the same perception of reality, the uniformity shapes our culture, how we relate to one another, and how we create future images.

Scholars debate how to define visual culture, when and where it began, and the best approach to learning about it. But we know that images have a secret language and history of their own, which must be uncovered to fully understand what they are communicating: their hidden assumptions, historical baggage, and problematic implications. We're learning how to uncover these from the scholars we cite in the book and those in appendix C, "Additional Resources," and we are grateful for their help. We hold ourselves accountable to them as we continue to learn. We begin here with these important lessons from white art critic John Berger's *Ways of Seeing:*

- The way we see things is affected by what we know or what we believe.
- Seeing comes before words and can never quite be covered by them.
- We only see what we look at.
- We never look at just one thing; we are always looking at the relation between things and ourselves.
- Soon after we can see, we are aware that we can also be seen.[32]

White writer Nicholas Mirzoeff also comes from an art history background but claims our visual culture has matured beyond such things as paintings and sculpture to now encompass visual events, through technological advances such as the Internet. Scholar Lisa Nakamura speaks to the power relations and racial formations that exist between subject, object, and viewer or user of images and visual media. In general, the field of visual culture studies has grown out of art history, aesthetics, cultural studies, performance studies, and cinema and media studies.

Have you had an immediate emotional response to a picture? Maybe it was the sight of a loved one who died, and the photograph of their smiling face or candid body language hit you like a gut punch of surprise, joy, and grief. Or maybe you've seen an image in the news that caused you to feel hurt, angry, or offended. And sometimes images evoke a sense of awe, wonder, and inspiration. Drawing from current research and methodologies, we can look critically at the acts of seeing and witnessing. We can take into consideration the ways that spacing, captions, or mixed media within an image impact its message. We can examine its invisible or overlooked parts to discover their meaning.

White author W. J. T. Mitchell puts it this way: "Vision and visual images, things that (to the novice) are apparently automatic, transparent, and natural, are actually symbolic constructions, like a language to be learned, a system of codes that interposes an ideological veil between us and the real world."[33] In other words, there is more than meets the eye.

Photography, in particular, is often seen as neutrally capturing reality. However, photography has never been a politically neutral endeavor. From its inception it has been used as a weapon against oppressed groups, as a tool of othering and stereotyping. It is "a key tool in visualizing colonial possessions and demonstrating superiority over the colonized."[34] One of its early "scientific" uses was to capture the physiognomy of different races to support arguments justifying slavery. We'll talk more about this in chapter 3.

What is our responsibility, then, as viewers? How can we ethically engage with images? Who can or should produce images? We must investigate why visual communication is so powerful. Further, learning about historical symbolism and meaning can help us better understand how and why multiple perspectives exist.

We don't usually know the motivations of the creators of the images we view. Yet, regardless of those motivations, when images draw on racist assumptions that reinforce stereotypes, universalize groups, or naturalize hierarchical relationships, they can promote disrespect and mistreatment of real people and the narrowing of their options. Our experiences shape what we can and can't see. Most white people have never thought about who gets represented in images and how, because we've almost always been represented in the images that we see, and in flattering and/or complex ways.

CREATING YOUR TOOLKIT TO CHALLENGE WHITE WAYS OF SEEING

In order to become aware of and question white ways of seeing, we need several things. Throughout this book, we provide components that make up a toolkit for you to challenge white ways of seeing. The first is reliable methods for analyzing images. We also need a lot of historical context, knowledge, and background to help us interpret images in the present. Finally, our understanding of images is underpinned by many codes and conventions. Your understanding and awareness of these codes and conventions will form the rest of your toolkit.

Codes are technical tools that are used to communicate an idea. For instance, imagine you are watching a film in which someone is home alone and the lights are out. The soundtrack offers a shrilling violin. The shaky camera follows the person down a dark hallway. As they turn their head, the camera zooms in for a close-up of their face. We know what will happen next: something horrible and probably gory, most likely a murder. We know this because the tools of camera angle, music, and lighting have been used in a convention that we understand.

While the codes alone can convey a message or emotion, we must examine them within a specific context in order to fully grasp their meaning. Typically, several codes are combined in a *convention* to create a commonly understood message. Conventions are sometimes rules that suggest a certain narrative or story. So, for instance, the horror movie example combines the setting, the lighting, the camera angle, and the music to create the convention of the climactic moment.

Such conventions may be more identifiable in movies and television than in still images. Conventions in pictures and photographs act in different ways and have different meanings, their histories have often been lost, forgotten, or ignored, and they are frequently not understood today. However, they often contribute to white ways of seeing. When we bring a historical understanding to visual conventions, we start to notice the racist and white supremacist messages and symbolism being communicated. Think back to the Dove advertisement discussed in chapter 1, which reiterated the convention, seen over many decades of US history, that Black people's color could be washed away by soap. By identifying the codes and the conventions being used, we can start to recognize them in everyday images. Here are some common ones, although of course these lists are not comprehensive.

TECHNICAL VISUAL CODES:

- lighting
- scale or depth of field
- framing
- arrangement of objects or subjects in the image
- camera angle or height
- shot selection (close-up, medium shot, etc.)
- page layout
- use of white space or negative space

SYMBOLIC VISUAL CODES:

- props and objects
- setting, scene, or context
- dress, style, or appearance of people depicted
- point of view the image takes on
- body language, pose, and facial expression of people depicted
- composition
- relative positions of people and objects
- color
- hierarchy of objects or people in the frame

Some viewers will analyze these codes out of interest in an image creator's artistic choices. However, our goal is to understand how they play out in racist visual conventions. We will explore the visual conventions, or generally accepted uses of technical and symbolic codes, that we see and use, but whose racist origins we don't usually recognize. We'll provide examples of how they work and discuss how they contribute to white ways of seeing.

There are visual conventions about many groups, just as there are stereotypes of many groups. Because of our focus on white ways of seeing, we'll explore conventions about a small number of groups, but in depth. And of course, we constantly create new conventions, combine them, and draw on existing ones for new reasons or in new contexts. Analysis of them could go on forever, but our goal is to provide a starting point.

Finally, a note on ethics and triggers. In order to teach you the visual conventions, how to detect them, decode them, and not perpetuate them, we include numerous images—examples of real advertisements, fashion spreads, journalistic photos, social media posts, and so on—to help you build your toolkit. However, some of them may be difficult or uncomfortable for you to look at. You may feel strong emotions and visceral reactions. You may think it was unethical of us to select certain images over others, to dissect one subject or model and not the millions of others we could have chosen. We did struggle with the question of whether it was necessary to include the actual images, or if we could simply describe them. Ultimately, we feel that you need to see them in order to understand the visual conventions at play. The pictures included in this book represent the larger visual conventions and patterns we are teaching. In addition, we do not mean to target or attack the individual photographers, models, brands, and labels depicted here.

QUESTIONS TO CONSIDER

Having familiarized ourselves with the social construction of reality, learned about ways of *not* seeing, and built up a toolkit, next we begin exploring how to become aware of specific white ways of seeing. But before we do, take a moment to reflect on all that was covered in this chapter.

- Have you ever found yourself in a situation like the one Liz was in when her friend posed with the statue? How did it make you feel? What did you do about it, if anything?

- What are some things, people, or experiences that have shaped your reality?

- Can you think of a time when you thought you understood a situation, but then someone pointed out something that you had missed? This could be a project at work, a news story, an event in someone's personal life, or something else.

THREE

REMOVING OUR ROSE-TINTED GLASSES

Representation and Black Women's Bodies

Images in our daily life are shaped by our culture and simultaneously shape it. When we first see an image, we're usually not conscious of all the assumptions, thoughts, judgments, and interpretations we bring to it. For example, if we're looking at a spread of fashion photography, we may assume that photographs are neutral reporters of reality, we may not notice how they normalize very thin bodies, and we may not be aware of how they draw on socially constructed beauty standards. These gaps in awareness affect how we think about ourselves and how we understand and treat other people. They lead us to see unjust systems as neutral and natural.

In this chapter we consider how people of color are exoticized, dehumanized, objectified, othered, and sexualized through certain visual conventions, focusing on Black cisgender and transgender women and girls. Different racialized groups are subject to different stereotypes and histories that shape the visual conventions targeting them. We go deeply into the case of Black women and girls, rather than providing a breadth of racial examples, to engage more fully with this group's complexity and to investigate the particular ways in which the lens of whiteness treats Black female bodies and people. And we acknowledge again that by reproducing these images we risk reexploiting the people in them—but without examples we can't teach you to challenge white ways of seeing.

You may notice that we named "transgender and cisgender women and girls" here, not just "women and girls." This is not because this is the only place we mean to include transgender people. We recognize that trans women are women and that trans men are men, and use the terms women and men accordingly. However, a person's cisgender or transgender status becomes relevant when commenting on the difference in how cis and trans people are treated. In these cases, we'll use the terms to identify which groups we're talking about. Otherwise, please note that we always intend binary gendered terms to be read inclusively.

This work is sensitive. It requires us all to be patient, with ourselves and each other, as we learn about our biases and discover how they both draw on and recreate the visual conventions underpinning racist images. To begin, let's explore the visual conventions of exoticism, dehumanization, objectification, and sexualization.

AN EXOTIC TROPICAL PRESENCE

"All set for summer? Turn up the heat with island beads, exotic floral necklaces, and juicy fruit charms," urges a headline in a 2005 *Teen Vogue* photoshoot (fig. 7).[35] Sounds like fun! The model, Moesha, is a thin, dark-skinned teenage girl wearing lots of colorful clothing (figs. 6–11). If we were flipping through this magazine in a checkout line at the store we might think, "There's a Black model—that's representation, right? And

Figure 6

Figure 7

that's good." Thinking about representation is important, but we need to look deeper. Remember, image-making is almost always political. Simply putting a person of color in the frame doesn't cancel out anything else that may be going on; we need to carefully analyze how the image works. It may be prompting us to unwittingly buy into racist stereotypes and hierarchies that in other areas of our lives we actively resist.

As we look through the article, we immediately notice an abundance of tropical flowers, fruit, and other items associated with the tropics. Moesha wears oversized fruit and flower necklaces, bracelets, and earrings. In one photo she wears a bathing suit with images of lemons and strawberries on it (fig. 7); in another, a shirt patterned with bunches of cherries (fig. 8). Her jewelry includes bananas and strawberries (figs. 6, 8, and 9) and lemon- and watermelon-shaped beads (fig. 6). In various photographs she wears a sun visor and platform shoes with tropical flower prints (figs. 9 and 10), a grass skirt

47

Figure 8

Figure 9

Figure 10

Figure 11

(fig. 10), a rattan necklace (fig. 6) and a bamboo necklace (fig. 7); she carries a fan-like rattan purse while sporting fingernails painted like a tequila sunrise (fig. 11). Her backdrops are bright yellow (fig. 11), purple (figs. 7–10), blue (figs. 7 and 8), and sunset orange (fig. 6), accessorized with a few tropical plant leaves (fig. 7), purple bamboo (fig. 8), and purple rattan (fig. 9).

While these items and colors may seem fun and innocent, we must realize that they have a history. Our white ways of seeing may tell us that this photoshoot is inclusive because of who Moesha is or appears to be: a Black girl. But we remember that we are probably not seeing the whole picture or story. What might we be missing? Consider the historical and cultural connections between tropical fruit and Black people.

Colonial histories and fantasies play out through visual conventions in Moesha's photoshoot. Fruit symbolizes abundance, and tropical fruit is often used to represent the "natural" fertility of the Global South. Fruit has also been used to represent stereotypes of Black people as fertile, lazy, promiscuous, and exotic. The bountiful tropics were assumed to allow Black people a leisurely life, and their "natural laziness" was used as a justification for slavery. Watermelon was associated with Black people's supposed "lack of self-control [and] child-like needs."[36] "Bananas were originally marketed as an exotic and novel fruit that signified tropical life. . . . The banana remains a potent signifier of economic relationships between colonizer and colonized, modern and primitive,"[37] and is still associated with promiscuity. When viewing the images of Moesha, we can begin to notice the racist symbolism that creates the visual convention of exoticism through the use of tropical fruit as props and on her body.

Let's also consider the use of other tropical elements, including flowers. Moesha is laden with tropical flowers, which are a metaphor for exoticness, lushness, and abandon (figs. 7 and 8). She is also photographed in a grass (mini)skirt (fig. 10). The captions and text reiterate the tropical themes, speaking of the "South Pacific," "tropical punch," "juicy fruit charms," and "United Bamboo." Moesha is presented as a desirable, exotic woman. We return to the ways Moesha is sexualized later.

The way that these images of Moesha suggest a carefree tropical island are reminiscent of representations of Hawaiian women (also stereotyped as "exotic"), who are presented as "always decorated with flowers, sexually available and unburdened by Western guilt."[38] In Indigenous Hawaiian (Kānaka Maoli) traditions and culture, hula is a highly skilled art form with deep, often religious, meanings. The raffia skirt or pa'u and flower crown lei or lei po'o are an essential part of those meanings.[39] Tourist culture, however, commercialized hula into what is now commonly referred to as the "hula girl." She is typically white or light-skinned, rather than having the darker complexion of many Kānaka Maoli, with long dark hair, and wears a grass (or cellophane) skirt and a bikini or coconut-bra top. Today, the hula girl can be seen on postcards, keychains, picture frames, t-shirts, dashboard dolls, and coffee mugs sold in shops throughout the islands. The hula girl imagery is grounded in white ways of seeing. It takes an aspect of Kānaka Maoli culture that is rooted in the importance of place, religious or courtly enactments, and resistance to assimilation and minimizes and whitewashes its meaning. Making the hula girl white or light-skinned, and then turning the symbol into capitalistic gain, like with tourism tchotchkes, dilute the cultural meaning and sacredness of the art. The hula girl trivializes and misrepresents Hawaiian culture while prioritizing the comfort of tourists.

As Noah Patterson Hanohano Dolim puts it, "hula kitsch" became a way to "promote Hawaiian culture without Hawaiians."[40] Nor does this occur only in images. The commercialized experience of a lū'au builds on and feeds into these exotic stereotypes. Getting "lei'd" with flowers while watching light-skinned dancers perform, tourists are once again "fed the images they expect to see" and the visual convention of exoticism continues.[41] (We discuss the creation of expected images more fully when we discuss Black Memorabilia, below.) These exotic hula girl stereotypes in images and tourist experiences have real-life repercussions. Scholar Julie Kaomea describes how imagery in Hawaiian elementary school curricula is eerily similar to that in tourist ads, depicting Kānaka Maoli as always welcoming white visitors, serving guests with generous hospitality.[42] Kaomea's work also reveals that Hawaiian schoolchildren often believe in the exoticized version of Indigenous Hawaiian culture. The kids describe Hawaiian women as really pretty and say that they wear costumes, play nice music, and are kind. When asked to draw a Hawaiian, some children drew a hula girl. Understanding the social construction of reality means we are not surprised by the results of Kaomea's study. But they are disturbing, and our understanding means we can work to counter the harm that seeing cultures through this lens of whiteness causes.

Looked at through a white lens, the tropical fruit and flowers that Moesha is pictured with in the photoshoot, the ways that she is dressed, Other her. The stereotypical image of the hula girl also Others Hawaiian women. What exactly is othering?

OTHERING THROUGH EXOTICIZATION

The Other is those groups or persons who are not (like) us. Othering denies the fullness of a person's humanity; it assumes the Other cannot live up to the ideal embodied by the dominant group; and it turns the person being othered from subject to object. When you are othered, "anything can be done to you."[43] Images of othered groups commonly suggest a hierarchy of dominance and subordination between "us" and "them." Of course, different groups are othered in different contexts. In a conversation about animal rights, animals would be othered; in a conversation about the experiences of Black and white male children in schools, the Black students would mostly likely be the ones othered. In our context, othering occurs because of white ways of seeing, so the Other is people of color, often Black people. Othering people stereotypes and excludes them, and it can be dangerous.

Othering also frames how we think about ourselves and who we imagine we can be. James Baldwin famously remarked, "If I am not what you say I am, then you are not who you think you are." A powerful reason white people demand that Others "stay in their place" is that we do not want to admit that we are not who we think we are. In fact, we project onto othered groups characteristics that which we dislike or fear in ourselves, such as emotionality and sexuality.[44] This also conveniently allows us to exploit or even exterminate the Other for possessing these supposedly negative characteristics.

But now we must turn all this upside down for a moment. In contemporary times, otherness is actually "in" and has become commodified. Exotic Others are seen as beautiful, alluring, sexy; they can be used to sell products. But that's part of the point we are making here. Using someone's ethnicity, race, and cultural symbolism to market items and make money is appropriation and exploitation. Exoticism is successfully used for capitalistic gain, bell hooks notes, because it offers a supposedly new, fresh, and more intense way of being, one more appealing than the "normal" or "dominant" lifestyle. She writes that "ethnicity becomes spice, seasoning that can liven up the dull dish that is mainstream white culture," but she fears that "the Other will be eaten, consumed and forgotten."[45] When images glorify the exotic Other as a means to gain followers, clicks, likes, and sales, they are offensive. It's also important to ask who is doing the glorifying—a member of the group, or a member of the dominant culture? We will discuss this more in chapter 5. We need to carefully analyze how images ask us to see people and objects from different backgrounds through a white lens.

When used as an excitingly exotic object, the Other can be hyper-visible—but the Other can also be invisible, a blank canvas that won't detract from the product being sold.[46] In a recent issue of *Vogue*, model Athiec Geng is portrayed with several aspects of otherness and exoti-cism (figs. 12–15).[47] In each photograph, she is alone. Like Moesha, Geng is not shown with friends or a partner. She appears to exist exactly as hooks feared: to be consumed and forgotten.

In the first image (fig. 12), Geng stands in what appears to be a desert. She wears a pink dress, white sneakers, and a tall white head-piece that has strands cascading in front of her face. She is angled slightly away from the camera, and we can't see her face clearly. In the second image (fig. 13), two pink shoes are suspended over her bare back. She becomes a literal backdrop, the high contrast between her skin, the shoes, and the blue sky intensifying the bright colors. In the third image (fig. 14), Geng is wearing a neon green suit with a tradi-tional Moroccan crown. The fourth (fig. 15) shows her in a bright yel-low dress with ruffles of pink, blue, orange, brown, and black. Draped over her shoulders is a traditional Moroccan wedding blanket in yel-low, and she wears a white headpiece that frames her oval face. In each of these photos, Geng becomes a "tabula rasa," or a blank slate, upon which the photographer, the fashion editor, and the clothing designers can paint. The title of the article is "Bright Ideas," referring to the neon-colored clothing that covers her, under which she herself fades into the background. She is like a mannequin in many ways.

Adding to this impression is her body language, which is quite different from that of most models. Rather than displaying a confident persona in vibrant poses, Geng lets her arms hang straight down, and

Figure 12

Figure 13

Figure 14

Figure 15

she looks at the camera with either no expression or a distrustful gaze. She is also not presented as conventionally alluring; for example, she is styled in sneakers rather than the high heels one expects in a fashion magazine. Though sneakers could be alluring, the almost straight-on angle and flat-footed poses defy posing conventions.[48] High-heeled shoes, of course, are one way women are sexualized. This photoshoot is an example of a person being exoticized without being sexualized; she is presented in a way that makes her fade into the background so the clothes are the main focus. In the next section we discuss ways that Others can be simultaneously exoticized and sexualized.

In short, exoticization is a visual convention that uses symbols, props, poses, and other tools to objectify or Other the person or people within the frame. Exoticization perpetuates white ways of seeing by presenting the Other as foreign, controllable, and consumable.

OTHERING THROUGH SEXUALIZATION

Othering people of color through exoticization can include sexualizing (and oversexualizing) them. We already know that women are portrayed in images, especially advertisements, as sex objects through conventions such as provocative clothing or even nudity, postures that convey submissiveness, facial expressions that communicate seduction, and image composition that centers and isolates traditionally sexual body parts. Minoritized racial groups are sexualized in particular and often more intense ways.

People of color, especially Black cisgender and transgender women and girls, are disproportionately associated with hypersexuality. They have often been stereotyped as sexually experienced "Jezebels" and "seductresses, a sexual predator of sorts . . . promiscuous and sexually irresponsible."[49] Beginning in slavery, Black women and girls were seen by white people as innately sexually immoral, which allowed white men to justify their own acts of rape and exploitation. Black transgender and cisgender women and girls have been unfairly associated with prostitution and seen as primitive and wild, as when fashion advertisements portray them made up and dressed like wild animals.[50] These sorts of images appear repeatedly, in multiple contexts, until they seem natural and we are unaware of their influence. Black girls are also seen as older than their actual age, as more sexually experienced and less in need of nurturing than white girls, which compounds the issue for them.

Social science research confirms that Black women are more likely to be dehumanized and sexually objectified than white women.[51] In one study, researchers tracked the eye movement of white American students (the majority of whom were female) looking at images of women. Half of the women pictured were Black, and the other half were white; some were wearing bikinis, and some were fully clothed. Participants shown images of women in bikinis spent more time looking at the breasts and groins of the Black women than of the white women.

Many Black women have been famously objectified for specific body parts: Sarah Baartman's buttocks and genitals, Josephine Baker's buttocks, Tina Turner's legs, Janet Jackson's breast.[52] Baartman was taken from her home in South Africa to be put on display in London as the "Hottentot Venus." Throughout her short life, Baartman was sold and traded among scientists and entertainers, her body parts studied and gawked at, and after her death she was dissected and compared to apes. Caricatures of her in newspapers and print flyers exaggerated her figure. Baker, Turner, and Jackson chose to become entertainers, but their work was and is sometimes overshadowed by commentary on and images of their bodies.

Photographers and editors use technical codes like cropping, framing, and lighting to convey different emotions and messages in the images they create. People who are highly valued are more likely to have their entire body depicted; white ways of seeing find nothing problematic with the convention of reducing others to body parts. Context is eliminated from the image and most of the body of the image's subject is cropped out. People so shown—especially transgender and cisgender women and girls of color—are objectified and dehumanized, "because they are not shown as whole persons. Hence, women are not presented as intelligent and active persons."[53]

Look back at an image from the *Teen Vogue* photoshoot that shows Moesha from the hips down (fig. 10). She is posed with one leg turned sideways, her knee bent and heel lifted to open her thighs. She is dressed in a shiny pink and red grass miniskirt which exposes her upper thighs and, at the end of a long expanse of bare legs, red tropical-print platform shoes, three or four inches high, that strap around her ankle. She has a bright red pedicure. A lavender wall, covered with yellow latticework that looks like a chain-link fence, and a concrete floor are visible. The photo caption is headed "Petal Pusher."

If we're seeing through the lens of whiteness, we assume there is no meaning here beyond fun summer fashion. But given what we know, and remembering the context of this image, how else might we read it? The cropping of this photo draws the eye to Moesha's bare legs. The short skirt and platform heels suggest "hooker" attire. The grass skirt references the exotic Hawaiian hula girl. The caption and background suggest that she is standing outside. When we put all these things together, we might read this image as portraying Moesha as a prostitute standing on a street corner. Indeed, bell hooks similarly describes the African model Iman, in a 1989 *Vogue* article, as "displayed as the embodiment of a heightened sexuality . . . she is naked, wearing only a pair of brocade boots, looking as though she is ready to stand on any street corner and turn a trick."[54] In the absence of any other narrative context, Moesha is presented as sexually experienced and available for the viewer's use and pleasure.

A second example of the convention of reducing people of color to body parts is figure 8, in which Moesha is bisected vertically and cropped at hip and shoulder, with her hand on her hip. The photo's center is the diamond-shaped space formed by her bent arm and the inward curve of her waist. She wears a cherry-print shirt tied at her waist, chunky fruited bangles and flower bracelets, and a ruffled bikini bottom. Moesha is sexualized here, not only because her hip and waist are visible, but because most of her body is cropped out and the curve of her torso is the focal point of the image. The hand-on-hip pose also suggests the Jezebel stereotype.[55] Overall, these two photographs suggest forward, aggressive sexuality.

Focus on disconnected body parts dehumanizes subjects not only by sexualizing them, but also by racializing them. These often happen together, but not always. In the March 2021 edition of *Elle* magazine, in a seven-page spread on style (figs. 16–19, 21 and 22), we see an unnamed Black female model cropped to show either her legs, torso, or chest.[56] The one time we see her whole face, she is looking down and pulling a hat down over her forehead (fig. 16). In another, we see only her chin and mouth, the latter highlighted with bright red lipstick, while the rest of her face is cropped out (fig. 17). The focal point of the image is her left arm, held close against her chest as she clutches two bags. A third shows her in a typical model hands-on-hips pose, but only from chin to mid-thigh, with the rest of her body cropped out (fig. 19). In an image that shows her torso and legs only, the gold chains of a Dolce & Gabbana purse are wrapped around her knees, as if binding them together (fig. 21).

Unlike the other photoshoots we've examined, this one does not name the model. She is not sexualized, but she is nonetheless another tabula rasa. We don't see a lot of her body, both because of the cropping and because most of her skin is covered by her (mostly) loose clothing

Figure 16

and accessories. The necklines are high and in one image depicting her legs and feet, her white stockings and chunky heels even suggest a prim sort of churchgoing character (fig. 18). She's not being portrayed as wild or animalistic. She comes across more as timid (in fig. 16, where she's pulling the hat over her eyes) or even frightened (in fig. 17,

Figure 17

where she is hunched forward, clutching the two bags). Finally, her fingernails are unpainted, which is unusual in a high-fashion magazine shoot where long, highly glossy and nails with colors or patterns relevant to the shoot would be expected. This lack further desexualizes

Figure 18

her, especially given that the animalistic sexualized Black woman stereotype is usually depicted with brightly colored, clawlike nails.

Rather than being sexualized, the model is being racialized here. The most obvious indication is her lipstick, which looks like a refer-

Figure 19

ence to common blackface minstrel images, such as those shown in figure 20.[57] The minstrel performers darkened their skin and used red (or sometimes white) paint to exaggerate their lips. Minstrel shows were developed in the early nineteenth century by white performers who "blacked up" using burnt cork or paint and caricatured Black people in front of white audiences, drawing on common racist stereotypes. "Blackface was racist in a very specific way—a way that allowed white people to define what it meant to be Black. It wasn't just painting with a Black brush that which was white, it was systematically performing Blackness through a white lens, with the intent to mock, to discredit, to minimize."[58] The damage has lasted generations.[59] In the *Elle* photoshoot, the first image showing the model's lips offers almost nothing to contextualize or balance out their vivid color: her other makeup is understated, her hair is covered with a bucket hat, and the rest of her body is cropped out, except, again, her unpainted nails (fig. 16). In the second, her entire face above her lips is cropped out (fig. 17).

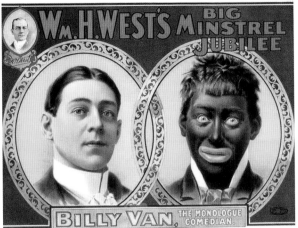 

Figure 20

Beginning in the eighteenth century and continuing into the mid-twentieth, a vast amount of domestic objects and ephemera depicting and referencing Black people and Black culture was produced in the US. These items are now called "Black Memorabilia," and they are often racist, offensive, and dehumanizing. They served much the same purpose as blackface: to persuade people that "Blackness is as whiteness sees it."[60] A Black Memorabilia figurine mirrors the stereotype the *Elle* photoshoot suggests, including the model's bright red lips and even her bucket hat (fig. 20).[61] Perhaps the creators of these modern images are not consciously aware of these histories, but we can read them in the images nevertheless.

The Mammy is another stereotypical image of Black cisgender and transgender women, and she often appears in Black Memorabilia, especially on kitchenware such as cookie jars.[62] Unlike the Jezebel, the Mammy is a devoted servant, more concerned about the white family she works for than her own. She is desexualized, usually portrayed as fat and dark-skinned, with African features.[63] You can see why this stereotype would be appealing to white people.

Scholar Rosetta Quisenberry, presenting racist Black Memorabilia postcards mailed by white people, shows that the banal, loving, or joking messages on them demonstrate no understanding of the violence perpetuated by the images on the reverse side.[64] She juxtaposes those images with dignified Black self-representations, sometimes formal studio portraits, letting these images "speak for themselves." She is showing her readers what we can see via multiple and contrasting standpoints, as we discussed in chapter 2. More importantly, she reveals the ways that the racist stereotypes don't seem to perturb white people, but definitely don't fit with Black people's images of themselves.

This historical context offers an additional perspective on the racialization of the *Elle* model. The image of chains across her knees harkens back to slavery (fig. 21). A plethora of other chains are featured in the shoot; in one photo she wears chain earrings (fig. 16), and in the centerfold, both her wrists are wrapped in chains with an additional chain-like bracelet on one arm (fig. 19). The photo in which chains lie across her legs is the only one in which she seems both racialized and sexualized. She is lying on a red floor and seen only from the waist down. We can see the curve of her hips, and her outfit, while heavily patterned, is more form-fitting. Her ankles are showing, and her high-heeled shoes reflect a sexy aesthetic. She is lying down, not in a position of agency or strength, and her legs seem bound in two places by the chains of the almost-invisible purse on her thigh.

A pattern of sexualizing and racializing by cropping and framing images in ways that reduce the photographs' subjects to body parts while also echoing blackface, Black Memorabilia, and slavery is a complex example of white ways of seeing. We white people often overlook, minimize, or ignore the ways that subjects of such photos are dehumanized, othered, sexualized, and racialized, as well as the ways that each of these forms of objectification reinforces the others. But,

Elle STYLE

GOOD AS *gold*

IN NEED OF A LITTLE SUNSHINE? AREN'T WE ALL. NO MATTER
THE WEATHER, CHANNEL ITS GOLDEN GLIMMER BY
INTRODUCING METALLIC FINISHES VIA CHAIN STRAPS,
LUSTROUS MATERIALS AND SHIMMERING EMBELLISHMENT

Shirt, £1,224,
trousers,
£2,493, sandals,
£902, and bag,
£1,905,
all DOLCE &
GABBANA

ELLE.COM/UK MARCH 2021

76

Figure 21

with intention and awareness, we can begin to notice these things that were in front of us the whole time. Seeing echoes of slavery in a fashion magazine definitely gives us pause; as we said earlier, it's important to learn to be comfortable with being uncomfortable, and this is another reason we suggest mindfulness practices in chapter 6.

Figure 22

WHEN THE MODEL IS WHITE

Let us compare how these Black women are sexualized, othered, exoticized, and dehumanized with the treatment given some white models. In the same issue of *Teen Vogue* that includes Moesha's photoshoot, another one, titled "Making Waves," instructs, "Get the crew together and hit the beach."[65] The narrative of friends enjoying a beach day is enhanced by the photographs of surfboards, beach blankets, games, blue water, and lush tropical vegetation (fig. 23). The white girls wear tropical-print bikinis, which reveal more skin than Moesha's outfits, and yet they are not particularly sexualized. This is because the shots include mostly full-body images rather than ones cropped to focus on body parts. The girls are photographed in a relevant context, so their attire makes sense; they are dressed for their (innocently fun) activities. Because we understand where they are and what they are doing, they are not positioned for consumption by the viewer. The spread includes separate images of items being sold, so we don't confuse the models with items for sale. The images of the white models also perpetuate white ways of seeing.

Meanwhile, as noted, the models of color in the other images we looked at are not shown as connected to others; they are not involved in any context or activity, and the selling is happening on and through their bodies, rendering them more available for the reader's consumption and subtly reinforcing their association with prostitution.

"Okay," you might say, "but it's not fair to compare two different types of photoshoots! Moesha and the unnamed model in *Elle* are not photographed on location, so what do you expect?" So let's look at a white model in a similarly decontextualized studio photoshoot showcasing brightly colored outfits, jewelry, and accessories (fig. 24).[66]

Figure 23

Figure 24

Fashion model Mona stands in front of a white background and wears clothing more subdued and loose than Moesha's form-fitting outfits. We see mostly feminine patterns and shapes like polka dots, hearts, and bows, which connote innocence. The images are cropped, but in a way that centers the products more than Mona's body parts. We could certainly dig into the gender stereotypes associating girls with bows and hearts, and the gendered implications of some of her poses, but our concern here is unlearning white ways of seeing. The images of Mona may utilize gender stereotypes, but nothing here connects to racist stereotypes and ideology, appropriation, dehumanization, or othering, as the images of the Black models did.

In one photo, we see Mona's forearm covered in chunky beaded bracelets. She's reaching down to attach a flower pin to the back of her shoe, which rests on a white platform. Her shoe is a woven flat, and her lower leg is visible. Contrast this shot with the one of Moesha's grass skirt, long bare legs, and platform heels (fig. 10)—and also with the one showing Geng straight-on, in an unattractive flat-footed pose (fig. 15).

In other images, Mona's face is fully or partially cropped out of the shot, but text like "Stock up on strands of juicy, jawbreaker-size beads," "Hard Candy," and "Good 'n' Plenty" places the focus on consuming the products, not the model.

In short, the Black models were exoticized, othered, objectified, and sexualized in ways that the white models in similar shoots were not. While all the images may seem neutral or unproblematic at first glance, racist visual conventions continue to circulate through and affect our culture.

A BETTER WAY

Does this mean Black transgender and cisgender women and girls shouldn't be photographed, can't be models? No, it means we need to recognize the problematic ways certain groups are portrayed and lift up the photographers, designers, and creators who are doing things better. Take for example the wife-husband team behind CreativeSoul Photography. Kahran and Regis Bethencourt describe themselves as visual storytellers whose "mission is to shatter the current standards of beauty and disrupt cultural norms."[67] Their website and social media showcase their dynamic photographs of children and families of color.

The clothing, hair, and makeup in the portraits take an Afrocentric perspective and highlight the authenticity of their subjects (fig. 25). In their AfroArt series, for example, the Bethencourts "aim to empower children of color to embrace their natural curls and the skin that they're in."[68] "Our hope is that Black children (and parents) look at these photos and see themselves represented in ways that they have not seen before."[69] The Bethencourts are primarily concerned with validating those featured in these complex, positive images and those viewing them, but those of us stuck in white ways of seeing can learn from their photographs as well.

Consider the framing, cropping, and styling of these images. They do not use the visual conventions we've analyzed throughout this chapter. The subjects in the Bethencourts' images are represented with dignity. Their entire face and torso are included, and sometimes their whole body; there are no close-up shots that dismember the people in the frame, sexualizing or dehumanizing them. The images suggest complexity, variety, playfulness. The use of studio photography neither isolates nor objectifies the individuals being photographed. There are no racist symbols used as props, accessories, or patterns.

Figure 25

Symbolically, the Bethencourts disrupt our visual perceptions of time, including the past, present, and future, combining a revisionist history and a hopeful view of tomorrow within a single photograph. Through their styling of clothing, hair, makeup, and props, each person is portrayed in a way that symbolizes Afrocentricity and Afrofuturism. Their work shows how images can be created from a different perspective.

Jari Jones (her first name is pronounced "Yar-ree") is another artist whose work is changing the narrative. A Black transgender woman, Jones made headlines in 2020 when she alone graced the highly coveted Calvin Klein billboard in New York City. The photo features Jones looking straight into the camera (fig. 26). Her shoulders are tilted slightly, while her head is squarely balanced and centered. She is shown from the chest up, against a bright blue backdrop, wearing a black top with the words *Calvin Klein* printed in rainbow colors on the right side. Though she is wearing red lipstick, this image is far from echoing blackface. Her red lips are not exaggerated, and her more glamorous eye makeup balances the look. Her coloring and outfit also are not those of blackface caricatures. Because we see her whole face and upper body, it is easier to see these differences. The studio setting doesn't Other, exoticize, sexualize, or dehumanize Jones. In an interview with *Bazaar*, Jones stated, "The photographer I've shot with many times, Ryan [McGinley], is a dear friend of mine. . . . And there were so many . . . so much diversity on staff. A lot of queer people, a lot of people of color. . . . And I think for the outside people who don't necessarily identify with the identities that I align with, it gives them a sense of possibilities of what our society can look like."[70]

Jones reminds us of the importance of intersectionality, as well as the danger of othering. And she challenges the visual convention of the Mammy previously discussed: she is portrayed as desirable and

Figure 26

with agency; her energy goes to her own activism, her communities, and the young queer and trans people of color who look up to her. She notes that the fashion industry has "never strayed too far from a tall, cis, thin, White, eurocentric structure. . . . it wasn't until the last 5 years that the fashion industry has substantially shifted."[71] Jones notes her own shifts as well; she has had to work through internalized fatphobia grounded in dominant assumptions. She celebrated her Calvin Klein billboard with a tweet: "Today, on #JUNETEENTH2020 a Fat Black Trans Woman Looks over NEW YORK !!!"[72] and she notes, "It was important for me to put 'fat' up there . . . so people know a fat body is worthy of celebration, it's worthy of love, it's worthy of respect. All those intersections, of being fat, of being trans, of being Black, it needs to be seen and named directly."[73]

An interview with Jones was *Teen Vogue*'s cover story that September (fig. 27),[74] and the images of her on the cover and in the article contrast strongly with the magazine's images of Moesha that we analyzed earlier. Jones's entire body is shown in the cover image, so that the viewer can read her body language, posture, and facial expression all together. In several images we see her looking right at the camera, sometimes serious and sometimes smiling and laughing. There are no

Figure 27

racist symbols used as props or decor. She wears in turn a cream dress with green bears printed on it, a yellow dress, and a pastel dress with geometric shapes. One photo adds a black leather jacket and Doc Martens boots; in another her dress is topped by a black coat with small floral designs (not tropical flowers, and with no fruit). None of the images suggest the tabula rasa effect we saw with Geng. The images were taken by Quil Lemons, who describes his photography as "a distinct visual language that interrogates ideas around masculinity, family[,] queerness, race, and beauty."[75]

Jones's work, done in collaboration with photographers, stylists, designers, and producers, indicates how images can be created and presented against the lens of whiteness. The more aware we are of visual conventions and their histories, the more we can unlearn white ways of seeing. But it's also crucial to see images that reflect new, more liberatory possibilities.

The images we analyzed in this chapter have multiple meanings. Maybe you noticed the presence or absence of things that we did not mention. You may have come up with different interpretations than we did. That's great. We now need to reflect on those—and when we say "we," we mean us authors as well! We are by no means perfect antiracist coconspirators. No such thing exists! Maybe in your eyes we made mistakes or missed something. The key is to have a conversation about these reflections, rather than move quickly to judging, controlling, dominating, or defending them.

We must continue to second-guess our initial reading of an image and consider other meanings, ideologies, or narratives that emerge from it. And when we look at an image multiple times, maybe coming back to consider it later, we may see things in it that we didn't notice at first. Challenging white ways of seeing means looking at the complex ways in which images work and the implications they have both for those who are depicted and for those who are not. We create our social worlds through communication, so we need to pay attention to what we are creating and interrogate the history, meanings, and implications of the images that surround us daily.

As we continue to unpack white ways of seeing and try to see differently, we can take what we've learned here and add it to our toolkit. You should also add your own questions, concepts, and thoughts to the kit. Going forward, we can all think about how white ways of seeing often miss problematic and racist stereotypes and representations of people of color, especially Black transgender and cisgender women and girls.

QUESTIONS TO CONSIDER

The next time you are scrolling through social media or flipping through a magazine in a checkout line, ask yourself the following questions:

- What do the details in the photographs reveal, and what racist undertones remain hidden?

- From whose point of view was each one taken, and who is meant to see it?

- What meanings or symbols are apparent in it?

- How do the framing, focus, cropping, and any historical allusions influence the way you interpret it?

- Are there visual conventions of exoticism, othering, dehumanization, or sexualization at work? How can you tell?

FOUR

ON A PEDESTAL

Masculinity, Race, and Threat

White ways of seeing encourage us not to notice racialized representations of people of all races and genders, and in all contexts. Last chapter, we explored how Black cisgender and transgender women and girls in the fashion and modeling industry are othered or sexualized in a racialized way. Similar things happen to Black cisgender and transgender men and boys, who are often depicted as aggressive, hypermasculine, or animalistic (among many other stereotypes). It's not enough just to be aware of the need for diversity of representation. Our white ways of seeing may see representation of diverse bodies and jump to the conclusion that "everything is good," but this often isn't true. We may be glad to see Black men on magazine covers, for example, but we have to make sure our white lens is not encouraging us to blithely consume a racist image.

SOME PROBLEMATIC ASSUMPTIONS BEGIN WITH COLONIZERS

In 2008, basketball superstar LeBron James appeared on the cover of *Vogue*, the first Black man to do so in the magazine's 116-year history (fig. 28). The cover photo shows him dribbling a basketball with his right hand while holding fashion model Gisele Bündchen in his left. He seems to be yelling or screaming, looking straight into the camera while Bündchen smiles. His body language looks active, tense, and aggressive next to Bündchen's windblown hair and supple posture.

The photograph is problematic because of its similarities to King Kong movie posters. Many versions have been made of the story of a giant ape who barrels through New York City, taking a half-naked Fay Wray as his prize. But the fictional King Kong was preceded by the "Mad Brute." The other image in figure 28 is a 1917 Army recruiting poster in which the Mad Brute, representing Germany, is carrying away Lady Liberty. The cover photo of James and Bündchen looks like it was taken detail for detail from this poster—especially James's color and clothing, facial expression, arm positions, and stance. Even his white-toed shoes echo the Mad Brute's lighter-colored toes. There are fewer exact parallels between Lady Liberty and Bündchen; Bündchen's expression is different, and her arms are in a different position. But her dress is very similar to Lady Liberty's, though her chest isn't fully exposed.

The LeBron James image draws on and reinforces ideas of Black men as animalistic, and particularly as apes or monkeys. This portrayal is one of the ways in which Black people have been dehumanized by white people for centuries.

Centuries ago, Africa was held in high esteem by Europeans. In the Middle Ages, the African continent had large kingdoms and even empires; moreover, much of East Africa had been Christian since the fourth century, and Europeans looked to it to help contain Islam. In West Africa, there were Islamic centers of learning such as the university at Timbuktu. Located in present-day Mali, medieval Timbuktu "became one of the major cultural centers not only of Africa but of

Figure 28

the entire world." Africans traded widely—Somalia, for instance, had diplomatic relations with China—and African societies welcomed travelers. Africans sat for paintings by Rubens, Rembrandt, and Van Dyck.[76]

But in the 1600s, European scientists, travelers, and philosophers began to see Africa as wild and her people as savage. White scholar Jan Pieterse makes the point that "there were drastic changes and differentiations in European images of Africa which were related mainly to changes which took place *in* Europe."[77] They were due not to Africans themselves, but to the desire and ability of Europeans to exploit African resources, force Africans into a capitalist system, and dehumanize those who would suffer because of it.[78]

In fact, many of the negative images were recycled: When the world of the English was much smaller, for instance, it was the Scots whom they saw as savage, and the Irish as wild and needing to be subjugated. The idea of the Wild Man and the links between denigration, subjugation, and exploitation reappeared later in Africa.[79]

Europeans had begun comparing Africans with apes and monkeys by 1699, on the basis of both physical features and "cultural" characteristics. Europeans created racial classifications based on the Great Chain of Being, "a hierarchical structure of all matter and life, with God at the top and minerals at the bottom," that dated back to the ancient Greeks.[80] While humans were the highest physical beings in the hierarchy, the ranking by race put Europeans at the top of the human hierarchy and Africans at the bottom, and therefore closer on the Chain to apes and monkeys. European scientists also speculated about a missing link between "Man" and apes. As you might imagine, all this was used to justify colonialism and slavery.

Figure 29 is a detail from "The Orang-Outang carrying off a Negro Girl," the frontispiece of volume 2 of the English physician and astrologer Ebenezer Sibly's *An Universal System of Natural History: Including the Natural History of Man, the Orang-Outang and the Whole Tribe of Simia*, published in 1795.[81] Here we see the European desire for Black women projected as a fantasy of actual relations between apes and African women.[82] The full image shows an African man shooting arrows at the orangutan and, in the background, the offspring of humans and apes. You can see that the posture of the "Negro Girl" is similar to that of Lady Liberty in the Mad Brute poster, though the orangutan seems to be a more caring captor, judging by his facial expression and body language.

Such racist tropes persist in our society and culture to this day. For instance, recent advertisements for toys and children's clothing have been called out for their racist messages connecting Black people to monkeys. The Lil' Monkey doll set, created by the Brass Key company

Figure 29

Figure 30

and originally sold in Costco, combines a Black baby doll with the name Lil' Monkey on her hat, a stuffed monkey, and monkey-related items, including a stuffed banana, monkey rattle, and bib.[83] "Diaper fits both baby and monkey!" exclaims the packaging (fig. 30). And an advertisement for clothing brand H&M shows a young Black boy modeling a hoodie that proclaims him the "coolest monkey in the jungle." A white boy, by contrast, is labeled "official survival expert" and "junior tour guide" (fig. 31). After public backlash, the ad was removed and the monkey hoodie pulled from the market.[84]

The difficulties with the King Kong–like image of LeBron James include not only its creation and publication at all, but also the fact that it was chosen for the magazine's cover. Remember, this was the first time a Black man had ever appeared on the cover of *Vogue*. Other images from the photoshoot were used in the article, and any one of them could have been chosen for the cover instead. Figure 32 is one of them, and figure 33 shows James on the cover of *GQ* nine years later. When you've finished reading this chapter, think about the different histories and implications of these images.

Figure 31

Figure 32

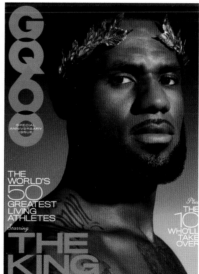

Figure 33

Given the images we've presented so far, you might be thinking that unlearning white ways of seeing requires primarily examining images of people of color. Actually, that's not the case. We are just as influenced by the portrayals of white people. White people, especially mainstream white men (the dominant group in our society), are often depicted positively and as the universal norm. If we don't know or remember that reality is socially constructed, we accept these depictions as true.

So let's now look at images of such men. To narrow our focus, we'll concentrate on images of white men associated with management and with diversity and inclusion in the workplace. Having become aware of how Black men and boys are often portrayed, we can see that white men and boys are often depicted as the exact opposite: as civilized, worthy, rational, and innocent.

HIERATIC SCALE

We begin by introducing another long-standing visual convention: hieratic scale. Hieratic scale is a way of indicating which people in an image are most important or most powerful, by showing them as higher, larger, further forward, more active, or more clothed than others. The word *hieratic* comes from the same root as *hierarchy*: hieratic scale is a visual code that tells us where people fit in a hierarchical system.

In Diane's city of Syracuse, New York, people recently lobbied for a statue to be removed from public view. The statue includes a large figure of Christopher Columbus as a young man "looking toward the west, maps and charts in his hand."[85] He is standing on an obelisk, and under his feet, on the four corners of the obelisk, are the faces of four Native Americans (fig. 34).[86] White historian James Loewen, author of *Lies My Teacher Told Me: Everything Your American History Text-*

book Got Wrong, could have been speaking of this statue when he said, "Sculptors typically place Native Americans lower than European Americans in historic monuments. Whites always wind up in positions of power and action while people of color are passive at the bottom."[87]

As a webpage about the statue put it, "Masks of Native American faces function as

Figure 34

clasps to hold the four sections of the obelisk together, and celebrate the people who were already in America when Columbus arrived."[88] A locally published pamphlet calls them "blankly staring faces in fanciful headdress."[89] It is certainly fanciful; those depicted on the sculpture look nothing like the headgear of the people indigenous to the Syracuse area. For example, traditional Haudenosaunee dress for men includes headgear, called gasdó•wä•', made from wood and specific feathers worn in distinct positions to indicate the wearer's nation.[90] Instead, the Columbus statue depicts stereotyped, generic "Native Americans," erasing the people of the Onondaga Nation on whose unceded lands Syracuse is built.

Even worse, the fact that the faces are masks has a terrible backstory:

These blank faces are not symbolic conquered cultures but the imagined faces of the dead. Throughout the 19th century, plaster casts made from dead and captive living Native Americans were a coveted commodity in museums and anthropological collections. . . . In this context, these grisly faces on the monument are simultaneously trophies, attempts to subjugate and symbols of domination.[91]

Of the Arawak people he encountered on his first voyage, Columbus asserted that "with fifty men I could subjugate them all and make them do everything that is required of them."[92] In fact, on his second voyage to America, Columbus did forcibly control, murder, enslave, mutilate, and rape many Indigenous peoples. As of this writing, the statue remains in Columbus Circle despite efforts to have it removed.

Now you analyze one. How is hieratic scale being used in the statue of Teddy Roosevelt in figure 35?

The African American and Indigenous men are much lower than Teddy Roosevelt. He is riding a horse; they are walking. He is front and center, taking the lead; they are behind him, passively following. And they are (by Western standards) half naked, while Roosevelt is in full uniform. Roosevelt's great-grandson himself argues that this statue should be removed: "If we wish to live in harmony and equality with people of other races, we should not maintain paternalistic statues that depict Native Americans and African Americans in subordinate roles."[93]

It may be clear that the same concerns apply to Confederate monuments, whose removal has also often been urged in the last couple of years. The cultural consensus on who is worthy of being commemorated in public memory has shifted, and many people in the group whose worth was never before questioned are, as a 1994 article put it, "white, male, and worried."[94] Some see efforts to remove statues and other monuments as attacks on American tradition, history, and heroes.

When we question white ways of seeing, we pay attention to arguments for removing statues, as well as those for other changes, such as

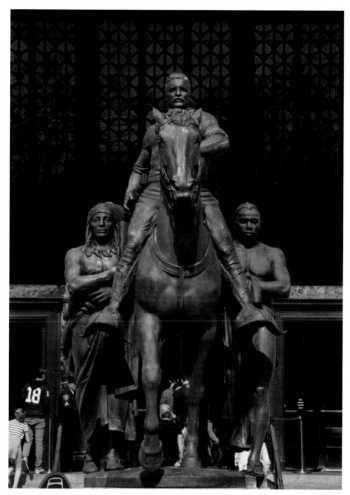

Figure 35

replacing sports team names and mascots that are offensive to Indigenous people. However, changing the way we see doesn't mean that
only the things we see (like statues or sports team mascots or logos)
need to change. Unlearning white ways of seeing can help us be aware
that broader systemic change is needed and motivate us to work
toward it.

SACRIFICIAL MAN

Hieratic scale appears not only in monuments but also in print images, blogs, and social media. It is often used to place white men on top as leaders, but it can also do other things, even within a single image. To illustrate this complexity, let's examine a drawing of an imagined statue, representing a figure we will call Sacrificial Man (fig. 36).[95] His dress shirt and tie, together with his short haircut, make him look like a white-collar worker, perhaps a manager. He is carved only from the thighs up; the marble below his thighs is an uncarved block. Six small Others (five men of color and one woman who, judging by the color of her hands, is white), also dressed in white-collar business shirts and ties, chip away at his thighs and the uncarved block with hand tools. We assume that the large male figure represents the white male dominance that structured organizations in the past (and continues to do so in the present) and that the Others represent the challenges to white male dominance presented by an increasingly diverse workforce. The range of people represented in management is particularly narrow, so *Others* here refers to those who are not male, white, cisgender, able-bodied, straight-passing, and young or middle-aged.

The Others are much smaller and lower than Sacrificial Man. While the convention of hieratic scale would usually mean that he is on top and has the most power, that may not be the case here. Sacrificial Man is being wounded by the Others, who chip away at his legs and his foundation in an attempt to bring him down. Interestingly, Sacrificial Man is passive, with his hands behind his back. His pose is very different from that of Teddy Roosevelt in the statue we analyzed earlier. Roosevelt's muscles are taut, his right arm cocked back and right hand tense and engaged; he is ready for action. Sacrificial Man's sad and stoic facial expression suggests he is mourning his personal

DIVERSITY

THE WHITE MALE:
An Endangered Species?

Historically positioned at the top of the heap, the white male is getting a taste of what some call reverse discrimination. How fair is it?

BY RENEE BLANK AND SANDRA SLIPP

Here in the United States, white, European, physically able, heterosexual men have traditionally defined the workplace norms and standards by which all other group members are judged. Some of those standards have been affected by the socialization of white men to be physically strong, competitive, aggressive, direct, dominant, knowledgeable and emotionally restrained. But that was then. This is now.

The 1990s are a transitional time for gender roles in our society. Women truck drivers and executives seem like an anomaly to many in these changing times, with sex roles increasingly blurred. Many men—and women—have been socialized to assume that only men would hold jobs requiring physical strength and dexterity, and that only men were supposed to hold the superior positions in organizations. As diversity reshapes the way American businesses look—and work—the sense of loss and disorientation experienced by many white men

Being white and male has traditionally conferred automatic advantage. But today, now that women and racial minorities have joined the competitive pool, the reality is that it has become harder for a white man to compete for a job.

ILLUSTRATIONS: MICHAEL NG

Figure 36

loss while understanding the need for sacrifice and organizational change.

We can bring other interpretive tools to bear on this drawn statue, as well as hieratic scale. For example, the fact that his thighs terminate in a block of marble suggests the possibility that the artist didn't want to draw Sacrificial Man on a pedestal, as many statues are placed both physically and metaphorically—that is to say, overvalued. And the fact that Sacrificial Man's hands are behind his back could suggest that his hands are tied, meaning that he is metaphorically powerless. On the other hand, research on nonverbal communication suggests that having one's hands behind one's back can mean one is hiding something, so the pose can be read as indicating either passive powerlessness or hidden power.

Let's take a closer look at the small figures, whom we call chippers. The two at the top of the block, who appear to be light-skinned men of color, are making the most headway. One is about two thirds of the way through one of Sacrificial Man's thighs; the other is the only chipper shown sending chunks of marble flying. The chippers who are lower down and hammering on the block itself are the darker-skinned men of color and one white woman. The threat to Sacrificial Man appears to come almost exclusively from men of color; the white woman is the only chipper who appears to have made no dent in the marble. Overall, the image greatly underrepresents the presence in middle management of white women (who were the main beneficiaries of affirmative action), overrepresents that of men of color, and makes women of color invisible. Do we imagine that there have been five middle management men of color for every white woman at any time in the workforce since the 1970s? If drawn more recently, for the chippers to accurately represent the members of middle management in 2021 who were not white men, they would be three white women, two men of color, and one woman of color.[96] (We have been unable to find information on the proportion of middle managers who are neither men nor women: nonbinary, genderfluid, etc.)

In this image, hieratic scale can be used to justify multiple and contradictory interpretations. Is Sacrificial Man, so much higher and bigger than the chippers, not threatened by them? Or is he weak and in danger from their swinging sledgehammers? Let's look at some other visual conventions, including classical Greek and Roman ideals, to help answer those questions. We'll also consider the meaning of memorializing someone in a statue and the value of the color white.

The material and form of Sacrificial Man suggest visual codes associated with the values of classicism, including "stability, timelessness, tradition and ancient roots."[97] For example, classical architecture maps these values onto financial institutions in ways that are ubiquitous, though often unnoticed, in our culture (fig. 37). Materials

Figure 37

93

such as marble, which is expensive, durable, and often white, are used for both buildings and statues to convey their value. Personal characteristics that have been associated with classical architecture include "status, morality, and character."[98] Classical imagery signifies and honors (white male) Western heritage and visually reinforces the current power structure. Although he is not a Greek god, Sacrificial Man's worthiness and power is shown by all these elements.

This image of Sacrificial Man also has subtle positive connotations because of its white color. Not only is whiteness, as a racial category, highly valued in the West, but so is the color white. As Robyn Morris, a scholar of Asian Australian and Asian Canadian women's writing, puts it, white represents "goodness, superiority . . . fairness, beauty, light and heavenly resplendence. . . . The invisibility and purity associated with whiteness is a contributing factor in the designation of racial difference."[99] Traditionally, statues have also connoted permanence, stability, prosperity, continuity, and security, and they generally represent only people thought worthy of commemoration. This type of visual code more subtly implies the power and worthiness of the white man depicted compared to an overt symbol, for example a Confederate flag, to promote white supremacy.

So hieratic scale, material, and color all factor into how we interpret the image. Sacrificial Man appears at the top of the image and seems to be made out of white marble. When we look at how these elements work together, the chippers seem to be attacking not just an individual but "the Man" and everything the Man represents: tradition, classical style, Western culture, and whiteness as a whole. The fact that Sacrificial Man's facial expression and posture are stoic and reserved suggest he is the victim, passively and helplessly attacked by these shifts in culture. The image suggests that he isn't responsible for whatever happens next. It doesn't consider the possibility that diversity would help both the white organizational man and the organization overall. The image presumes a zero-sum game.

A hieratic scale with a passive person on top is a bit of a contradiction, and such contradictions indicate that something worth careful scrutiny is going on. In this case, perhaps the image is meant to be ambiguous about diversity in management. Or perhaps it was designed to avoid offending readers of the associated article, regardless of their ideology. There isn't one right answer. What is important is to consider the possibilities and to be aware of how our perspective may be shifting as we begin to unlearn white ways of seeing.

To practice doing this, and to gain more skill with the elements of your toolkit, consider figure 38, a more recent image that accompanies a 2020 article called "A Point of View: Confronting White Fragility and Male Fragility with Empathy."[100] It shows a white man, whom we will call Fragile Man, sitting in what looks like a meeting space in a white-collar office. He is leaning forward, looking at the camera,

Figure 38

arms resting on his legs and hands clasped in front of him. He is front and center, the focus of the image—and *in* focus, unlike the other people in the picture. The other people, presumably other office workers, are walking around in the background, smaller, and blurred. They also appear to be female and/or racialized: Black, Latinx, and Asian. Write down what you notice about this image.

Here's our take: Hieratic scale invites us to interpret Fragile Man, like Sacrificial Man, in multiple ways. He is larger and the focus of the image, while other figures are blurred; perhaps we are meant to understand him as dominant. But like Sacrificial Man he is passive, while the others are active around him, and he seems similarly serious and concerned. We read his facial expression to mean he's willing to give up his current advantage to create a fairer workplace.

What would it mean to use an image that decenters white men, promotes their giving up their current advantage, and highlights the positive aspects of an inclusive, diverse workforce? Have you seen such an image, or can you imagine one? The stock photos on sites like Getty, Canva, and iStock are used for everything from marketing to journalism, and these images often reflect and reproduce the same visual conventions we've been discussing. We may not give much thought when putting an image into our PowerPoint slide for a school or work presentation, but when we consider our white ways of seeing, it becomes clear that most images are far from perfect. And far from innocent.

When we are reading a blog or article, watching an advertisement on YouTube, watching a presentation, or perusing a company's website—and when we are creating any of these ourselves, and choosing or creating images to accompany them—we can notice how white ways of seeing may play a role in the choice and design of every image. Whether their creators mean them to or not, they speak volumes about how we perceive people on the basis of race, power, social norms, class, ability, gender, and so on. Even when they are meant to represent a diverse group of coworkers, many stock images show a white person centrally standing, speaking, or walking, thus implying that they are the group's leader (and also associating leadership with lack of disability). Other images use facial expressions and postures to show white people as unsupportive of colleagues of color, and some eliminate white people altogether.

Remember that white ways of seeing are like blind spots; our minds will often fill in what's missing. Now look at figure 39, a stock image that accompanies an *Inc.* article titled "Should You Ask Diverse Members of Your Team to Help Attract More Diverse Talent?"[101]

When Diane was looking at images of diverse work groups, she initially assumed that this photo was not a good example because although the people in the image are diverse in race and gender, they are probably all looking at a white male boss who is out of the frame. The main subject is seated and looking up, presumably at the leader

Figure 39

or manager speaking to the group. This positions the unseen boss in a higher physical position and status. But why did she assume that? Why did her mind fill in the missing boss with the image of a white man? Because she was looking through a white lens. White ways of seeing mean that we expect to see white men in such roles.

The next time you are looking at a picture of several people, see if you notice hieratic scale being used to depict power relations among them. Is a white male larger, taller, or more in focus than the others?

DISAPPOINTED MAN

Hieratic scale appears in many places and usually shows white men on top. This is one clear way in which images communicate that white men are worthy. Another way is how their emotions are depicted.

For example, the main illustration in an article titled "Are White Males Being Left Out?" is a photograph of an alabaster-white male mannequin in a suit and tie (fig. 40).[102] He is young and classically good-looking. We will call him Disappointed Man. The article discusses whether an organization can address white male concerns while still taking seriously the concerns of minoritized members. That Disappointed Man is suffering is clear from the tear rolling down his cheek. The cause can only be the open gift box in his hands, which contains nothing but tissue paper. The box is turned diagonally and appears to be

Figure 40

quite large, almost as wide as his shoulders. This image suggests that Disappointed Man is entitled to something that he formerly got, was still expecting to get, but is no longer getting.

Although men are often stereotyped as not showing sadness or vulnerability, Disappointed Man is crying. Moreover, the image is accompanied by a teaser for the article that reads, "If diversity programs are as effective as they should be, white males should benefit as much as women and minorities. Why then do they feel so left out?" also focusing on his sadness at being excluded.

Both the title and the teaser suggest that white men are under threat: that they are losing their rightful entitlements and benefit less than others do from efforts to increase diversity. White ways of seeing might encourage us to accept that without much thought. However, white men do benefit from diversity initiatives in many ways. They may receive individualized benefits, flexible work schedules, career development and coaching, encouragement to develop their full potential or to bring their authentic selves to work, or improved work-life balance. But the ultimate goal of diversity efforts is to change the balance of power between white men and Others. White men currently hold a disproportionate amount of power, so of course they will not gain as much when diversity efforts are successful.[103]

The image of the empty box (which is repeated throughout the article) suggests visually that white men are now getting less (or even nothing). It presents the situation as unfair and conveys that individual white men are threatened because of it. However, the article's title is in the form of a question, "Are White Males Being Left Out?" which allows some ambiguity. Perhaps they're not being left out. The teaser's question "Why then do they feel so left out?" also implies some ambiguity; maybe they aren't being left out, they just feel that way. Language, like hieratic scale, can allow for multiple interpretations.

One page of the article includes a series of three photographs of a middle-aged white
man in a suit and tie holding a
similar box. In the first photograph it is chained shut; in the
other two it is open and obviously empty (fig. 41). Why was
the mannequin replaced with an
actual man? Perhaps the actual
man still represents the universal
white man, just as the mannequin
did, conveying that all white men
feel the same loss and disappoint-

Figure 41

ment. The use of a real man in these images also humanizes his feelings, while images of people of color often dehumanize them. And the
fact that he's middle-aged might suggest that those who are not too
young and not too old have more to lose or are valued more.

The chains wrapped around the box in the first photograph symbolize the white man's belief that he is not able to access the things he
used to be entitled to. In the second image, he is showing the reader
the empty box with a disappointed expression, eyebrows raised and
frowning. In the third photograph he is holding the box upside down
as if to shake it and say, "There's nothing in here!" He looks at the
reader with disgust and concern about his situation. However, the
quotation under this photograph reads, "You become very pragmatic
when the ship you're sailing hits rough seas. You don't care who the
crew is. You want to know if they can save the ship."[104] The image
suggests the problem is that the man is threatened because he lost
something he should still have, but the quotation suggests the prob-

lem is organizational difficulties which can be dealt with by pulling together as a team, regardless of race and gender. It is also an example of colorblindness; "You don't care who the crew is" disavows any acknowledgment of difference.

Like Sacrificial Man, these images contain potentially contradictory elements, and readers must choose how to engage with them. Don't be lulled by interpretations that fit what you unknowingly absorbed growing up. Use your toolbox to ask questions and notice alternative possibilities. Carefully consider contradictions and ambiguities within images and between images and the surrounding text as you work with white ways of seeing.

WORRIED MEN

Another way images suggest that white men are worthy is by depicting organizational members who just happen to be very traditional white men. The lead image accompanying the 1994 *Business Week* article "White, Male, and Worried" shows eight men who look as though they are from the 1950s (fig. 42).[105] They are in their twenties to fifties, wear conservative suits and ties, and have old-fashioned glasses and haircuts. The suggestion of a time decades ago implies that those "good old days" (when people of color and white women were not vying for inclusion, especially in managerial roles) are valued and should be brought back. The men's faces surround a doorway that frames a much smaller Black man and a woman who could be read as white, but we read her as Latina because of her dark hair and eyes and high cheekbones. Drawing on our knowledge of stereotypes about women of color, we also read her as an angry woman of color because of her crossed arms. While we see the full bodies of these two Others, the white men are shown as faces or head-and-shoulders shots; and

Figure 42

while the Black man and Latina woman are clearly standing together, the white men are a collage of disconnected images of different sizes, not a group. Their separateness suggests that we should see white men as individuals and perhaps that they have "made it" on their own, not because of their group membership.

Hieratic scale is at play in this Worried Men image; the people in the doorway are smaller than the white men, indicating the white men's greater importance and worth. Five float above the people in the doorway, looking down at them. Several of the white men have stern expressions; several seem amused.

Showing the full bodies of the Others emphasizes their embodied nature. This might seem like a good thing, considering that in the previous chapter we discussed how showing a person as disjointed body parts is denigrating, and showing their full body is preferable. But here the disembodied white male heads visually suggest white men's supposedly disembodied and detached existence, their rational and intellectual nature, while the Others are embodied and therefore emotional and animalistic.

We've already discussed the long history of associating Black people with monkeys and apes, as well as how the *Vogue* cover photo of LeBron James echoed the screaming Mad Brute. The linkage of race with rationality on the one hand and emotionality on the other has a long history, including during the American Revolution: "Identifying white with rationality or mind, they [revolutionary leaders] associated peoples of color with the body. Thus mind was raised to authority over the other parts of the self, and whites were raised above blacks and Indians."[106] Furthermore, focusing on the faces of the white men here is different from focusing on depersonalized body parts we explored in the previous chapter. We can read the men's expressions and infer their feelings and thoughts by seeing their faces, but many of the fashion photographs we looked at in chapter 3 gave us no such access to the models' minds due to entirely cropping out of the frame the models' faces.

Toward the bottom of the "White, Male and Worried" image, the two younger men directly under the Others look up worriedly at them. Because the Others are "out of place," the younger white men below them may not be able to rise in the organization unimpeded, as they once would have. The white man shown largest, who is not only middle-aged but also spatially positioned between the younger men and the older ones, gazes directly at the reader, seeming to ask for outside intervention. The title "White, Male, and Worried" also suggests a looming threat.

Yet the minoritized people in the doorway are far to the rear, small, and standing in a doorway. It is unclear whether they will be allowed to enter. Doors "are critical markers of power, protection, status" which can literally and metaphorically separate insiders and outsiders.[107] The threshold is also a liminal space—an in-between space, one of possibility and of change. The white men dominate the foreground and are clearly entitled to control the space. All of these markers—tradition, size, and space—point to the worthiness of the white men, and it is the "worried" white men we are encouraged to sympathize with.

As with the Sacrificial Man image, hieratic scale can suggest an alternative interpretation of the image: It can be read as showing a small pair of Others surrounded by a much larger (in size and number) and menacing group of white men. The teaser quote seems to support this notion (against the article's title), since it reads, "As companies hire and promote more women and minorities, they feel a backlash from some white males."[108] But the "women and minorities" are shown only on the doorstep; they have not necessarily been "hired and promoted." Because of both their small size and their embodied nature, they may literally not "fit in." And, again, like the Sacrificial Man image, this image underrepresents the number of women managers.

Are white men still worried, almost thirty years after this article appeared? It would be nice to think that such problematic images are no longer disseminated. But we recently came across a similar image (fig. 43) illustrating an article entitled "These 8 Men Have as Much Money as Half the World."[109] Do your own analysis before you read the similarities and contrasts that we note below. Do you see hieratic scale being used? What's in the background? What message is this image sending about white men?

The image, like the Worried Men one, shows juxtaposed and individualistic floating white heads, with a range of ages, though these men don't appear particularly old-fashioned. They are more similar in

Figure 43

size to each other than the Worried Men are. The men in this image are not ordered hieratically by age. In the Worried Men image, the older men look down at the interlopers, the younger ones look up at them in alarm, and the middle-aged one in the middle looks to the audience for help, but here the men at middle top and middle bottom look toward the reader, and the three on each side are angled toward or looking toward the image's center. We read this convergence of sightlines as suggesting these men do their own thing individually, but at some level their interests are aligned.

Some things we still have questions about. The background of the Worried Men image is blank; what is the meaning of the background here? It looks like rows of safety deposit boxes. On the website where this article appeared, there is a flashing light at the top center of the image. It looks like a burglar alarm is flashing on the ceiling of the room behind them.[110] This sends the message that these men are stealing the

105

world's wealth. Finally, are these eight rich men worried? Their facial expressions depict many of the men speaking, with mouths open. Their expressions don't seem to imply worry or concern except for Bill Gates, in the lower righthand corner. Contrasting his expressions with the Worried Men image, he shares a furrowed brow with the largest man in the image. Yet Gates is not looking into the camera like his counterpart. Perhaps this suggests he is worried more about the other white men rather than another group or demographic. We can't know, of course, although we may be influenced by adages such as "more money, more problems." But certainly the image doesn't suggest that they, like the Worried Men, must cope with a threat posed by interlopers. And the converging sightlines suggest that they can rely on one another's support, which there was no suggestion the Worried Men could do.

At the time of publication (2017), these men—six white Americans, one Mexican, and one Spaniard—were the wealthiest men in the world. Because the image appears to consist only of white men, our white ways of seeing may suggest that wealth has nothing to do with race or gender. But race and gender profoundly influence how easy or difficult it is to get ahead.

All of the older organizational images we analyzed (Sacrificial Man, Disappointed Man, and Worried Men) suggest multiple interpretations of both the threat and the usefulness of racial and gender diversity in organizations. The more recent images we compared them with (Fragile Man and the Richest 8 Men) also contain ambiguities. We make these comparisons so we can notice changes over time, or lack of change, or even regression. The lure of the progress narrative is very strong and fits with the assumptions of white ways of seeing. For example, it's easy to assume that diversity must have improved substantially over time. We're not going to argue that one image and

Figure 44

one article can disprove this, but take a look at figure 44, from a 2019 article called "How to Show White Men That Diversity and Inclusion Efforts Need Them."[111]

Go back to everything we said earlier in the chapter about hieratic scale and Greek classicism, about statues, material, and the color white. Think about the particulars of the Sacrificial Man image. Does this new image represent progress?

Here's what we see: The article's title makes clear that the Greek bust represents white men. The little fluffballs represent people of color (and perhaps women) in the organization. This image is much less open to multiple interpretations than many of the ones we looked at earlier. The Greek bust accrues all the high value we mentioned earlier: He is classical; he is a statue; he is white. The size difference between the white man and the Others is much greater in the new image, and the Others here are not even actual (albeit small) people with some power and agency (as they were in the Sacrificial Man image) but small, harmless, nonsentient nonhumans—balls of fluff. Though the angle of the statue's head reproduces a common classical pose, he could also be interpreted to be "looking down" on the fluff-balls—the Others. The fluffballs' range of colors, few of which even approach the skin shades of actual people, even brings to mind the common colorblind exclamation "I don't care if you're Black, white, purple, or green" (although note that there are no black fluffballs).

Consider how much you've learned in this chapter by going back to the two positive images of LeBron James (figs. 32 and 33). What can you suggest about the James and Bündchen image now that you can draw on the idea of hieratic scale? How can you interpret the James *GQ* cover now that we've discussed classical imagery and how it conveys that someone is worthy and worth remembering?

Here is our analysis. Bündchen is much higher than James, but she appears more passive since she is leaning on him. Her stature (notice that even this language reflects hieratic scale) is thus both raised and lowered. The colors they're wearing are significant: James is in black, Bündchen in white. We've already discussed the meaning of the color white. In the West, black connotes evil, darkness, dirt, and pollution. Considering that Bündchen is so far above James, standing upright with her straight right arm seeming to press strongly down on him, we might interpret him as a pedestal supporting a valued white statue.

By contrast, on the *GQ* cover LeBron James is presented in a classical Greek style, humanized and portrayed as worthy of being commemorated. The gold laurels around his head suggest Greek athletic championship. Of course, gold is valuable, but this valuation still draws on and reinforces the narrowness of the range of roles that are stereotypically acceptable for Black men and boys: athletes or entertainers. While better than the Mad Brute image, the photo doesn't offer a complex or progressive perspective. Also, drawing on Western associations of white with goodness and purity and black with evil and pollution, James's skin is lighter and more brightly lit in this image. Finally, his countenance here is calm, reflecting the higher value placed on rationality than emotionality in Western thought.

As always, we encourage you to disagree with our interpretations, go beyond them, or take them in a different direction. In this chapter we've focused on some long-standing visual conventions: the association of Black people with apes and monkeys, and hieratic scale, which tells us who is powerful and valuable and who is not. We've added these visual conventions to our toolkit, along with information about classical monuments and the meaning of the colors white and black. We've looked more closely at how an image and its surrounding text can be interpreted in multiple, and sometimes conflicting, ways. We've noted that our assumption that things improve over time is not always borne out. Use your analytic skills to consider the images you see around you every day, and see if that is true in other cases. And remember that unlearning white ways of seeing also means learning to analyze images of white people.

QUESTIONS TO CONSIDER

- Do you ever use stock images, such as in work presentations or on social media? If so, can you analyze their use of racial hierarchy and power dynamics?

- Are there monuments in your community that you now understand to be problematic? Can you go to them and analyze them firsthand?

- Have you seen images promoting diversity, equity, and inclusion at work, at school, or in other venues that you now consider to be problematic? Have you seen ones that you think are good?

FIVE

THE WHITE SAVIOR SELF(IE)

Social Media, Branding, and Humanitarianism

So far in this book, we've shown you ways to analyze images that we see in our everyday lives. Now we are turning the camera lens around to ourselves. Many of us regularly create meaning by taking pictures and sharing them on social media. We realize that not everyone uses or has easy access to social media. But to talk about unlearning white ways of seeing we have to talk about social media because it impacts the way we think about the world and the way we understand, and therefore treat, people.

During college, Liz studied abroad for a semester in South Africa. Her program focused on community development and service learning; students partnered with local nonprofit organizations in the impoverished townships that surround the city of Cape Town. Liz's work involved creating and leading programs for children ages five to fourteen. While there, she took pictures of the kids, the program staff, and volunteers as they played sports, did art projects, and participated in team-building activities. In one image, Liz holds in her lap a young girl who is wearing Liz's sunglasses (fig. 45). Liz posted these pictures to Facebook and her blog and used them in a slideshow she presented to her church when she returned home.

Figure 45

People don't think critically about the act of taking a picture, including a selfie, and posting it online. It is a popular way to show ourselves in a particular place at a particular time. It tells a story of who we are. But we may not be aware that a picture, taken in a certain context with certain people and posted in a certain setting, can reveal our white ways of seeing.

Have you ever taken a selfie, decided you didn't like it, then proceeded to take more until you had one you liked? Many of us have done this or seen friends or family members doing it. We want to see ourselves in a certain way, and this influences how we do in fact see ourselves and how we act. We also want other people to see us in a certain way. We curate our image on social media in order to convey to others and to ourselves that we are the person depicted. But, as we know from our work with white ways of seeing, it's more complex than that.

Research suggests that when we post online, we are engaging in self-branding, deciding how to perform our online identity. We are creating a persona to be seen both by others and, crucially, by ourselves. Liz's picture with the young South African girl created Liz's persona as a global volunteer, approachable and friendly to all. She took the picture as a way to capture the memory of the moment, but posting it online was a way of communicating who she was, both to others and to herself.

We make and remake ourselves. Ironically, we curate our image in order to appear real and authentic. Social media is designed to be a space of self-branding, so it's nearly impossible to post anything without branding ourselves in the process.

For instance, if we see ourselves as generous and caring, we may want to help people in need. Maybe we decide, like Liz, to volunteer, donate to a charity, or work for a humanitarian organization. Posting images of ourselves "helping" reinforces our self-image and the values we hold. That sounds fine, right? As you will discover in this chapter, there are ethical concerns involved in how we see and present ourselves. The ways we use visuals to communicate our self-image can be counterproductive and even harmful. We are going to help you learn what these concerns are, so that you can avoid using images unethically.

To do that, we examine images posted on social media and what they imply about white ways of seeing ourselves. Keep in mind that these are only a few examples of a larger issue. Our analysis here can also be applied to photographs we take but don't share online. And of course there is no quick fix for the problems we discuss. This chapter is intended to help you fully comprehend the problem; we will offer suggestions for how to address it in chapter 6.

For you to fully understand the research and analysis in this chapter, we need to address the methodological and ethical background of this work. The topics we explore in this chapter—white saviorism, cultural appropriation, and missionary and volunteer tourism—can be found across many social media platforms, in many contexts and from many perspectives. To keep things manageable, we investigated a specific genre of social media posts where each of these topics emerge:

humanitarian images posted by Peace Corps volunteers (PCVs) and Christian missionaries on Instagram. Of course, this is a narrow scope, and we must remember that many people do not have the economic privilege to do such work. However, the visual conventions that appear in these posts are found on all social media platforms, in images created and posted by people with all levels of privilege. As we explore the examples below, we ask that you apply what you learn to the media you consume and the images you produce.

We reviewed over two thousand images posted on Instagram between 2017 and 2019 tagged with #HowISeePC, a hashtag used by PCVs serving all over the world. We also reviewed over a thousand images posted in 2020 and 2021 tagged with #missiontrip, #missions, and #missionstrip. These images are accessible to the public and are representative of the larger discourse of humanitarians, voluntourists, missionaries, and international development workers. We selected the images that we analyze here on the basis of how they reflect white ways of seeing, and we discuss them in detail, including the captions, hashtags, and comments associated with each post.

It is important to note that not all PCVs or missionaries are white. Nonetheless, the majority of them, regardless of skin color, are prone to producing images using white ways of seeing. Also, of course, different social media platforms are popular at different times and among different groups; as we write this book, many people are shifting from posting photos and text on sites like Instagram to posting short videos on TikTok. The analysis we demonstrate here can be used on videos as well as still images, regardless of platform.

Turning the lens around on ourselves and drawing on the social media posts of everyday people requires a somewhat different strategy than earlier chapters. While we still describe in detail the images and associated text that we analyze, we don't include those images. We do not wish to vilify or incite violence toward the people who took the pictures, who appear in them, or who posted them. We did include several of Liz's own photographs, used to illustrate particular codes and conventions.

Since we show few images in this chapter, we suggest that you go to your favorite social media sites and search some of the hashtags mentioned in the images we analyze. Find your own examples and use the chapter as a guide to analyze the codes and conventions you see playing out as we go along. You already know a lot about white ways of seeing, so start your own analyses from the beginning of the chapter. This will give you a head start on applying what you learn to the media you consume and the images you produce.

WHITE SAVIORISM AND SELF-CENTERING

We are not critically analyzing international volunteering or humanitarian service itself. Rather, we are interested in how the pictures people share of such actions reveal how they see themselves, and in particular how the images reflect and are influenced by the idea of the white savior. *White savior* is a term used to criticize white people who complacently see ourselves as doing good, coming in from outside to help others, while being unaware of both the ways that racism is embedded in our motivations and behavior and the negative effects that they have. Critiquing white ways of seeing means examining how we see ourselves, how others see us, how we document our lives in pictures, and how we share those pictures with others—and it also means understanding why, based on all that, other people may question whether our "helping" work actually helps people. Challenging white ways of seeing ourselves requires being open to understanding how and why other people may not see us the same way.

Author Teju Cole describes the white savior complex as an ongoing reality for Africa especially:

> From the colonial project to *Out of Africa* to *The Constant Gardener* and Kony 2012, Africa has provided a space onto which white egos can conveniently be projected. It is a liberated space in which the usual rules do not apply: a nobody from America or Europe can go to Africa and become a godlike savior or, at the very least, have his or her emotional needs satisfied. Many have done it under the banner of "making a difference."[112]

White saviorism focuses not on the pursuit of justice but, as Cole writes, on "having a big emotional experience that validates privilege."[113] It concentrates on the white person's journey and transformation, emphasizing their selflessness and the risks they take for a worthy goal—which is, of course, achieved in the end. It perpetuates the myth that white people can "save" people of color and that they are entitled to do so as they wish.

We begin our analysis with what is probably the most popular kind of picture on social media: the selfie. Selfies tend to be the easiest genre in which to identify white ways of seeing, because in them we are centering ourselves. Layla Saad describes white centering as "the centering of white people, white values, white norms, and white feelings over everything and everyone else."[114] In selfies, we focus on our perspective and our transformations, even while documenting our service to others.

For example, consider Peace Corps volunteers. Since 1960, thousands of Americans have served communities overseas in the areas of education, healthcare, agriculture, environment, and economic development. Each year, three or four thousand new volunteers enter the

Corps and are sent to over sixty countries around the world. They go through intensive cultural and language training, and the large majority of assignments require a college degree. We might assume that this work is exhausting and never-ending, as volunteers must balance the daily demands of their host community with the country's general economic, healthcare, and education needs, as well as probably facing culture shock and homesickness. And yet the images we find on social media tell a very different story.

Many Instagram posts tagged with #HowISeePC offer a smiling selfie accompanied by a caption in which the PCV describes themselves as happily "living their best life," and include emojis such as sunshine, rainbows, and stars. The captions are almost "cutesy," representing the volunteers' identities, bodies, and experiences as pure, fun, and innocent, and their work as natural, positive, and effortless. Whether they actually experience their work this way is impossible to know, and also not the point. What matters is that they make the effort to portray it this way. They monitor themselves, choosing their body positions and facial expressions and crafting their captions and tags to reinforce both how they see themselves and how they wish other people to view them.

Liz similarly documented her time in the Peace Corps through selfies, although she did not post them on the social media of the time. Figure 46 shows Liz on her first night in her host family's house, standing in front of the white wall of her bedroom. She also took pictures of herself on vacation at Lake Kivu with fellow PCVs and sitting in her rural community's health center toward the final months of her service. In each of these she is smiling, presenting herself (to herself) as happy. But she was in emotional and mental distress when each of these was taken. Those feelings were not to be documented or displayed in photos. Although she did not share her photos, we can trace visual

Figure 46

conventions playing out in them—conventions that we continue to see today in the #HowISeePC Instagram posts.

Several selfies tagged with #HowISeePC similarly show PCVs as happy but also somehow nonchalant, as if being a humanitarian in a faraway country is no big deal. For example, a volunteer in Tanzania poses in the doorframe of her house, with a brick wall in the background and natural light brightening her face. She looks straight into the camera with a smile, wearing no makeup; her blonde hair rests upon her shoulder. The caption reads "Curly hair, bricks, and comfy track suits. Home. Also, this is me, the person behind the camera and dog ears :). Karibu Tanzania! . . . . #pcv #pcvlife #intentionalliving #pctanzania #howiseepc #wanderer #wanderlust #africanadventure #traveller #peaceofmind #brickhouses #tracksuitlife #thisisme #thisiswhoiam." Here, white ways of seeing influence how she sees herself in this role and how she wishes her audience to see her.

The post acts to brand its subject as a Peace Corps volunteer, a humanitarian, a white savior in a way that looks natural, calm, and peaceful. The role of a PCV is to serve others and be in community with them, so using a selfie to illustrate filling that role is a prime example of how our actions reveal white ways of seeing. If we want to document our development work, or any kind of project or service, why not show images of the actual work? There was in fact a brief trend on social media of people posting before and after shots of their efforts at picking up garbage in public spaces, promoting environmental awareness by announcing how many bags of trash were collected. Showing the work you've done tells a story of your usefulness and educates your followers about the needs you've tried to meet. The selfie, on the other hand, focuses on the individual volunteer. White ways of seeing encourage us to produce images that frame us, literally and figuratively, as central, when what is truly important in the situation has little or nothing to do with us.

We found similar selfie images and nonchalant descriptions across many of the missionary images as well. It's estimated that more than two million American Christians go on short-term domestic and international mission trips each year.[115] Americans spend an estimated $2 billion per year on international mission trips of a year or less.[116] White ways of seeing are also reflected in selfies featuring the volunteer surrounded by Black or Brown children. Although these images include other people, they are primarily about the volunteer and their experience. Our culture makes it easy for us to picture ourselves this way. After all, celebrities doing humanitarian work are shown this way too: think of Angelina Jolie talking intimately with refugees in Pakistan, Bono walking with schoolchildren in Lesotho, and Madonna holding an orphan in Malawi.

Consider for a moment the visual codes that appear in these images. Most of the children are smiling. The selfies are zoomed in, squeezing faces into the frame, and the contrast between the white face at the center and the darker faces surrounding it is substantial. The volunteer often looks joyous. The images suggest that the volunteer has recently experienced, realized, or understood the lives of impoverished youth for the first time.

Further, the captions continue to center the volunteer's voice, experience, and perspective. Volunteers may identify the children by name or role and may say something about them. More often than not, though, the children go unidentified and serve only to spur emotions in the volunteer, who may describe themselves as feeling touched, overjoyed, and in love. Some posts ignore the children in the image completely and discuss something unrelated in their captions. When trips were canceled or postponed in 2020–21 because of the Covid-19 pandemic, many former missionaries and PCVs posted images of themselves with children on previous trips to describe how much they missed the work.

Liz's selfie with the young South African girl reflects the codes and conventions discussed here. And it wasn't the only such selfie she took. Because of her white ways of seeing at the time, she didn't question herself when she was taking the pictures or sharing them with others. However, when she learned more about privilege, white saviorism, and visual communication, she understood that taking and sharing these pictures was self-centering and self-serving. It's certainly natural to focus on ourselves in posts to our social media accounts. The problem is when racial power disparities are also displayed and reinforced.

In these images, the relationship between light-skinned and dark-skinned bodies is on display. The innocence, vulnerability, and joy of the children become a trope for the volunteer to use to brand themselves as a compassionate, caretaking white savior. This trope is not new.

While mass media images of humanitarianism, such as in news coverage of wars, famines, and refugee crises, have tended to use white ways of seeing that focus on the pain and suffering of others from the viewpoint of a witness, social media images insert the photographer into the frame, posing them in a positive moment with Others who are impoverished and assumed to be suffering. The Others are used for self-serving, self-branding, and self-transformational purposes, in ways that both reinforce and center white supremacist thinking. As Saad writes, "If you unconsciously believe you are superior, then you will unconsciously believe that your worldview is the one that is superior, normal, right, and that it deserves to be at the center."[117] Note that she specifies "unconsciously." Becoming conscious of these beliefs is one step in changing the script, decentering the self, and unlearning white ways of seeing. Meditation can help with this, and we give detailed information in chapter 6 to get you started.

Centering the self is a predominant convention of white ways of seeing and white saviorism. The story we are telling is about us, and the voices are ours and ours alone. Many others have analyzed this pattern in movies and books. Kelly J. Madison, for instance, writes about how "antiracist white hero" films, such as *Amistad*, *The Help*, *The Long Walk Home*, *Mississippi Burning*, *The Blind Side*, and *Freedom Writers*, perpetuate white supremacy.[118] These films define white supremacy as extreme and distant, focus on the "good" white person's experience over that of the person of color, and construct a paternalistic view of racial struggles for equality. They shape not only our collective memory of particular events and our social history, but also our interpretation of the present.

The narrative of antiracist white hero movies communicates white innocence. It portrays "a 'diversely human' whiteness that diffuses guilt, and, in benevolently superior relation to blackness, reaffirms the legitimacy of white domination and identity."[119] Over time, the notion of an antiracist white hero became so normalized that we failed to see the implicit racism it perpetuated. It showed us how to behave in a way that we thought was progressive, selfless, and promoting diversity and inclusion. So we incorporated those behaviors uncritically into our lives and into the images we create and share. But upon deeper reflection and education, we can understand that centering the self means decentering those we claim to be serving or helping. Instead we are helping ourselves, not to mention often distorting history.

CULTURAL APPROPRIATION

Seeing ourselves through the lens of whiteness takes many forms. In addition to centering ourselves within an image, we sometimes "try on" attributes of different cultures as a way to show our appreciation and recognition of difference. For instance, we may adopt traditional clothing or hairstyles. There are more and less problematic ways of doing this, so let's explore both.

Dressing like the Other can be a form of cultural appropriation, which writer Ijeoma Oluo defines as "the adoption or exploitation of another culture by a more dominant culture. This is not usually the wholesale adoption of an entire culture, but usually just attractive bits and pieces that are taken and used by the dominant culture."[120] In the PCV and Christian missionary posts we examined, dressing in clothing that is customary for the culture and people the posters are serving sends a particular message. Sara Ahmed notes that "identity is reconstituted in an intimate relationship to 'the strange' and the exotic. The Western consumer is invited to 'go ethnic' through what she or he might eat, drink or wear."[121] The volunteers and missionaries are suggesting, through the images they create and share, that they are not merely engaging with the local culture as tourists, but have assimilated. They present themselves not just with Others, but as Others.

This self-presentation erases the racial, cultural, political, and societal relations of power between the people and cultures involved. The images ignore the privilege and entitlement of the PCVs and missionaries, suggesting that their compassionate willingness to become Others might even establish equality between them. Ironically, the PCVs and missionaries are the guests and the minority in the situation, but their hosts are still the ones being othered.

Of course, this isn't always the case. When Liz was in Rwanda, her host mother gave her a traditional Rwandan dress and headscarf. She invited Liz to put them on, showed her how to wrap the headscarf properly, and asked to take pictures with her in the backyard of their home (fig. 47). Refusing such an offer of cultural education and exchange could have insulted her host family. On another occasion, a friend and coworker invited Liz to be a bridesmaid at her wedding. It was an honor and a privilege to be asked, so she accepted. Like the other bridesmaids, she wore a brown satin wrapped dress, with a belt and necklace made of woven straw, and a small bead on a ribbon around her head. Liz posed for many pictures that day. She participated fully in both the wedding and the moment with her host mother, and she showed the pictures to friends and family when she returned to the US and could explain their context and background.

Posting such pictures on social media, however, involves a high risk of cultural appropriation. Viewers don't have the full story or the

Figure 47

context and may not read any contextualizing information that is offered, such as in the captions. They may perceive the poster to just be presenting a curated self-image.

Some people do indeed post images this way. For example, a PCV in Panama posted nine photos that she described with the caption "Spent an incredible week in the Emberá-Wounaan territory of the Darien Jungle eating wild rabbits, dancing, parading, and playing games. What an unforgettable experience with amazing people. #howiseepc #peacecorpspanama #cuerpodepaz #emberá #wounaan." The first image is of her with someone who seems to be an Indigenous Panamanian man. The volunteer is dressed in Indigenous attire and has patterns painted on her light skin. The man has similar patterns on his brown skin, and he wears a green headband, made of what look like coins, and a small beaded covering at his waist. The two appear to be standing in a bamboo structure, and bunches of green bananas can be seen in the background. The caption does not mention this man; it offers no name, title, or explanation of his relationship to the volunteer. We can only assume he is one of the "amazing people" mentioned in the caption.

In one of the other photos, the volunteer poses with another female PCV, the two of them smiling at the camera. They are dressed in brightly colored floral-print skirts and beaded tops, their white skin is painted with dark lines and shading, and the poster is wearing beaded earrings. The poster and her friend are "trying on" the traditions and dress of a different culture to see what they look like on them. Her post ignores the privileges that mark their bodies and allow them to move into this space freely; she is using this culture's dress and traditions to brand herself.

The other photos included in this post seem to represent Indigenous Panamanians with painted skin participating in various ceremonial activities. Young non-Indigenous people, presumably other PCVs, validate the uniqueness of the local practices through their participation, but ultimately it is the poster herself who is showcased. The other people are only props she uses to brand herself; the viewer can only speculate about who they are and why she is photographing them. Neither the Panamanian people nor the other PCVs have a voice.

The poster's audience is often also looking through the lens of whiteness, so they don't take issue with visual conventions that include cultural appropriation. Many viewers with white ways of seeing don't question the lack of context and see the photos as unproblematic. For instance, another PCV posted seven images that show her with her back to the camera while she dances with a group of Malawian young adults. The caption reads,

> I truly believe that until we can see each other as humans, as equals and all differences aside this world will remain the same. I believe

that simply based on religion, complexion, geographic location, or family upbringing we are all equals. I believe that sharing laughter and smiles is the easiest way to break down boundaries. So next time the opportunity presents itself, stand next to a stranger, share and smile, and if they dance . . . dance with them. ■🕊️🌍🐦 #howiseepc #peacecorpsmalawi @peacecorpsmalawi @peacecorps.

The two comments on this post say, "This is beautiful!!" and "Love the braid!" The central focus of all the photos is the PCV. Her caption flattens the material and socioeconomic differences between herself and the people she is surrounded by, ignoring the privileges and affordances that some have and others do not. The caption also reflects a colorblind mentality. Overall, the post is an example of seeing a community through a white lens and using it and its people to help our own brand. It is regressive, connecting to the ideology of white saviorism: if we white people will only believe that everyone is equal and relate to Others with smiles, laughter, and dance, we can change the world. This PCV is framing herself as a "global sister" and best friend to the Other. She blithely offers her own solutions (which aren't actual solutions) to today's global issues without any regard for how she is appropriating culture, ignoring differences between herself and them, failing to gain their consent to reproduce their images, and centering herself, or for how all this furthers the lens of whiteness.

The desire to be changed and inspired prompts these volunteers not just to interact with Others but also to take on their attributes. Ahmed writes that commodities represent difference and "can allow you to alter the surface of the body" so that the Other's difference "can become *your difference*."[122] Similarly, white scholar Sean Smith writes that "mimicking the lifestyle and/or clothing of a local resident often reflects a pursuit of authenticity," but people are appropriating the "identity of those who call the destination home, effectively claiming the destination (temporarily) as their home, too."[123] The PCVs in these images take on difference as a way to brand themselves and their journey as authentic, cultured, and global. It is an example of how white ways of seeing can manifest through behaviors that appropriate both individual acquaintances and entire cultures.

IMAGE FRAMING WITH COLONIALIST ROOTS

White ways of seeing can be found in how we frame our travel images and where we place ourselves within that frame. Almost three-fourths of Instagram users ages 18–30 claim to use it while traveling, and marketers claim that the platform is vital to the dreaming phase of travel planning.[124] A plethora of missionary and PCV images show the poster from the back, facing a vast landscape. For example, in one image a volunteer in Tanzania sits on a grassy perch overlooking a valley, with mountains in the distance and a bright blue sky with puffy white clouds overhead. In different countries, with different volunteers, this image is repeated over and over again. The accompanying captions tend to reference the volunteers' personal emotional and spiritual growth. In searching her own records, Liz found she had taken such a photo of friends during her time in South Africa (fig. 48).

Such a framing is so common in travel photography on social media that we may not question it. But through a critique of white ways of seeing, we can start to understand its negative connotations and colonialist history.

Photographers describe how back-portraits, in which no face is visible, allow us to imagine ourselves as the subject being viewed from behind. We can project our own perceptions, emotions, or memories onto the image. Alternatively, such a photograph may create a double

Figure 48

gaze, where we are watching someone watch something else.[125] In landscape photography, photographing an observer from behind takes on a unique and symbolic tone when documenting a moment. Rather than simply capturing a landscape or event, images of the back of a subject can almost "seem to speak more broadly, about the nature of things in a more timeless way."[126] It may, at times, help to convey tranquility, contemplation, or serenity.

What does this have to do with white ways of seeing? Well, there is a deeper history to framing a photographic subject as a small figure against a vast landscape. These images are using what Sean Smith calls the "promontory witness" trope, in which the human subject is shown as a "small and indomitable figure standing fearless against the epic scale of nature."[127] The spectacle of the landscape connects back to colonial paintings and photographs that depicted foreign lands as something to be dominated and acquired, and its people enslaved. Drawing on the work of W. J. T. Mitchell, a white scholar of visual culture, Smith writes that landscapes are "akin to the 'dream-work' of imperialism, where narratives of power and expansion are extolled through both metaphor and realist portrayals of conquered territory."[128] Eighteenth- and nineteenth-century depictions of the "exotic," "Edenic" Global South are notable for the "prevailing *vacancy* of the landscape"; its apparent lack of inhabitants allowed Europeans to imagine occupying it themselves.[129] When we show ourselves looking out over a "foreign" land, we evoke the horrifically exploitative practices of our white European ancestors. Like us, they looked for adventure and new sights, wondering how and where they might fit themselves into the landscape. Today, the messages that our images convey may not be those of traditional colonizers ("this is mine, a place for my future empire") but those of self-centering globetrotters and humanitarians ("look at me, in this exotic place").

Neocolonialism uses humanitarianism to mask its domination of formerly colonized countries. Whether the humanitarian volunteers themselves are conscious of that colonialist connection is unknown and irrelevant. Portraying ourselves looking out over an exotic landscape perpetuates white ways of seeing, because it communicates that we are not from that place yet are entitled to be there. The conventions of hieratic scale encourage us to interpret such images as showing us expressing dominion over the land. Social media is the perfect stage on which to brand ourselves citizens of the world, capturing in pictures the ways we transform and are transformed by the "foreign" landscapes in front of us. Yet, in doing so, we once again reveal our white ways of seeing.

OBJECTIFYING THE OTHER

Even when the photographs we take don't include us, we risk perpetuating white ways of seeing. In earlier chapters of this book, we critiqued white ways of seeing the Other in images from such sites as advertisements and fashion shoots; here we investigate them in images we take ourselves. White bodies can usually move through the world in safety, without giving thought to whether differently racialized bodies are watching. The visibility of racialized bodies, however, especially Black and Brown ones, is controlled by white supremacy. As discussed in chapter 3, they can be rendered invisible to white society, but they can also be made hypervisible—subjected to abuse, appropriation, surveillance, and murder. George Yancy defines the *white gaze* as the way white people perceive the Black body (or any nonwhite body) as suspicious.[130] The white gaze takes many forms; one you may be familiar with appears when white people claim to find Black people threatening, even to the point of calling the police, when they're just going about their ordinary lives.

In addition to Yancy's white gaze, which fears the racialized Other, white ways of seeing also include the colonial gaze, which acts to conquer or exoticize the Other, and another that we call the white savior gaze. The white savior gaze acts to use the Other as a photographic prop in branding ourselves as innocently well-intentioned.

For example, the missionary and PCV posts that center the Other often focus on the Other's labor and emotions, which the poster interprets or translates in simplified, sometimes patronizing ways. In a post by a volunteer serving in Zambia, we see an older Zambian couple standing outside in front of lush green trees and a bright blue sky. The man, on the right, wears a plaid button-down shirt, and the woman is wearing a headwrap and dress of African textiles. They are smiling widely and have their arms loosely around each other; he is looking up, and she is looking directly at the camera. In the caption, the PCV writes,

We spend every Tuesday morning with them. This was a beautiful moment, but I can't say she's always this happy. She usually tells long stories involving death and pain—she's lived a tough life. We've tried asking questions so she could recall some happier moments, which helps temporarily. The only time I've seen her this happy was when she began singing "I Want to Hold your Hand". We'll show up next Tuesday with an arsenal of music. Truly, they are two people I'll never forget.

The volunteer describes the uniqueness of this joyful moment by vaguely referring to the woman's pain. Then she quickly moves on to her own plans to create happy moments for her, while not really under-standing or acknowledging her unhappiness and what may underlie it. Is she just sad about her "tough life," or is she suffering from PTSD or mental health problems? In fact, we don't learn from this description what the volunteer actually does with the couple each week, or even what their names are. They are not given a voice or the agency to tell their own story; the PCV speaks for them and facilely comes to their rescue.

The white savior gaze sees the best in Others while remaining bliss-fully ignorant of its own racist and colonialist implications. False and even toxic positivity is dangerous in any context, but especially in a culture that is not one's own. It can make those entering the setting comfortable while enabling them to avoid addressing real issues. Posts such as this are a product of white ways of seeing. The volunteer com-municates her version of her relationship with the local people as a way to influence how she sees herself and to further her brand.

Another PCV, in Swaziland, photographed a four-year-old Black boy squatting down in front of a wall. His arms are wrapped behind his knees, and he wears sandals, blue jeans, a white tank top, and a black baseball cap that sits sideways on his head—clothes similar to what we might see Black children wearing in the US, or indeed anywhere in the Global North. The crisp whiteness of his shirt contrasts with the dusty ground he squats on. He seems to have been caught mid-laugh; his eyes crinkle with delight. He appears happy to be being photographed.

The caption reads,

> Everyone meet bhuti wami (my brother) Melo. I come home from classes every day to a flying hug, and him yelling AUNTIE at the top of his lungs. He's been my buddy since the beginning, and as my SiSwati improves, I'm finally starting to understand him when he talks. He's just as smart, sweet, and sassy as any 4-year-old I've ever known. I'll miss him a ton when I finish training and move to my permanent site. #peacecorpseswatini #howiseepc #g16simunye.

Other Instagram users commented on the post, writing "I just cried wow," "I NEED TO SQUEEZE HIS FACE HES SO CUTE," and "oooohh i love this sisi 😺."

The volunteer's description centers her side of her relationship with the child and what she gets out of it. She assesses the child's intelligence, sounding surprised that he is "as smart, sweet, and sassy as any 4-year-old." But why wouldn't he be? And both she and the commenters gush over his cuteness the way they might coo over a friend's new baby. But he is not a baby. His familiar style of clothing enables him to be read through American aesthetics of Blackness, while his youth and Africanness exoticize him in a way that averts the fear often implicit in a white gaze. Instead, we see him through the white savior gaze. The boy is visible in this frame, on this platform, connected to this user's account, frozen in time and space. It was the volunteer's choice to post his image. We don't know anything about him. As viewers, do we have a right to know? Do we even want to know? Did his family consent to this public posting of his image? When we look at images such as this, what are we focusing on: a brief moment of entertainment, or our self-image as global and inclusive? White ways of seeing prevent us from questioning these practices of taking and posting images because we are focused on ourselves, our brand, and how others see us.

Now it's your turn. If you haven't done so already, go to Google or your favorite social media platform and search using one of the hashtags we described in this chapter. Do you notice white ways of seeing in the images you find?

Although we've previously given our own responses to exercises like this, we obviously can't do so this time—but you, dear readers, are ready to fly on your own. In the images we *did* analyze, as usual, you may have noticed something different than we did, interpreting the post differently, disagreeing with our take, or going beyond what we noticed. Take another moment to think about what you noticed in the posts you found, and be ready to look for more filters, blind spots, and unfamiliar perspectives in your everyday life.

It's revealing that we speak of "taking a photo." We are taking something from someone or some place when we photograph them. Part of what we're taking is the person's control over their own image. We might use it in any way, including against their own or their group's interests. White scholar Susan Sontag compares photography with war, writing that "'shooting' a subject and shooting a human being" exist on the same continuum.[131] The images we've explored in this chapter (and the #HowISeePC hashtag itself) show that PCVs and

Christian missionary volunteers feel that their own privileged race, nationality, and positionality entitle them to capture photographs, and therefore to capture the bodies within them.

Of course, it is not just the production and circulation of these images that are problematic. The white savior gaze also relies on audiences to consume them. Ariella Azoulay argues that there is an "ethics of the spectator."[132] Audiences should pay attention to who is made visible and who is made invisible, whose voice is recognized and who is silenced. The posts explored in this chapter tell us a lot about the experiences and perspectives of the volunteers, but not much about the people they are supposedly serving. Our willingness to consume these posts and accept their images as unproblematic also says a lot about us.

YOUR WHITE LENS

Those of us who aren't traveling around the world in the name of international development, or consuming images posted by those who do, may think these examples have nothing to do with us. But think about other situations that you do find yourself in—situations where you think of yourself as giving back, contributing to the betterment of others. Do you serve meals to homeless people at your place of worship? Have you participated in a Black Lives Matter march or rally? Have you helped your kids do a clothing drive for school? Has your workplace offered a volunteering day or mentorship program to benefit "underserved" communities? As part of this or any similar endeavor, did you take pictures? Were any of them selfies? Did they include people who weren't with your group of helpers, but were in the group you were helping? Did you post any of these images on social media? Did you get the consent of the people in the picture both to take it and to post it? What did you say in the captions? Did you talk mostly about your experience: what you got out of it, what you learned, and how it emotionally impacted you? What was your motivation for posting it?

These are just some of the questions we must start asking ourselves if we are to challenge the lens of whiteness, unlearn white ways of seeing ourselves and begin disrupting the patterns of white saviorism, cultural appropriation, and unethical tourism. While pictures may seem harmless, it is important to critically analyze whose story we are telling and whether it is wise to do so. In the next chapter, we show you some steps to take, as both a consumer and producer of images, toward building antiracist ways of seeing.

QUESTIONS TO CONSIDER

- Look through your own photographs and social media accounts. Where do you notice white ways of seeing?

- On your next trip, how might you document your experiences and memories while being aware of the lens of whiteness?

- How might you talk with friends and family who continue to post images that are based in white ways of seeing?

- Where else might you find yourself perpetuating the lens of whiteness?

SIX

CONTINUING THE WORK

So where do we go from here? We've explored many visual conventions and codes that we encounter every day and that reveal the privileged views that continue to shape our society. Becoming aware of them is the first step, and that's what we've tried to help you do in this book. We showed you how to critically analyze and deconstruct the innumerable images we all consume and produce. We hope that you have started to see those images in a new way, more deeply and critically.

From here, it is up to you to decide how to move forward.

We did not write this book to make you feel guilty about your past usage, consumption, or production of visual images. Audre Lorde writes, "Guilt is only another way of avoiding informed action, of buying time out of the pressing need to make clear choices, out of the approaching storm that can feed the earth as well as bend the trees."[133] You have the ability, the power, and the privilege to take action right now. Guilt wastes time and promotes inaction—and inaction is a privilege, one that people of color have noted they do not have. If we are truly dedicated to working toward an antiracist way of seeing, we must commit to doing so, actively, throughout our lives.

NOW WHAT? BROADENING YOUR VIEW

Rachel Alicia Griffin, drawing on fellow Black feminist scholars Patricia Hill Collins and D. Soyini Madison, writes that "media does have the power to shape, influence, and suggest who people are and subsequently how they can acceptably be treated."[134] And we've illustrated that throughout this book. As white people, we can't simply read a couple books about racism and antiracist theory, join a book club (more on that later), pat ourselves on the back, and excuse ourselves from the duty to fight white supremacy and white ways of seeing. Broadening our view and interpretation of the images we see every day requires us to remind ourselves of our white ways of seeing again and again and again. We must mindfully shift our consciousness each day, each moment we encounter or create images. We need to constantly challenge ourselves to work against the deeply rooted racist conventions that shape how we perceive the world and the people in it. We must be committed to continuously recognizing, questioning, and unlearning white ways of seeing throughout our lifetime.

How can we do this? Remember the concepts we've introduced: the social construction of reality, intersectionality, and standpoint theory. We can remember that there are many, many standpoints and challenge ourselves to engage with more than just our own. We can read histories, personal stories, and analyses by people with different perspectives and understandings.

Standpoint theory helps us escape the trap of dualistic thinking, which is deeply ingrained in Western society (fig. 5). Questioning our first impression of an image is one way of challenging dualistic thinking. Embrace the complexity of multiple perspectives and multiple interpretations of images. Ask who or what is missing from an image. Are there complex histories that are being stereotyped, diluted, or misrepresented by it? (Some philosophies and religions also encourage us to consciously work to transcend dualistic thought.)

Awareness of interdependence also works to counteract dualism. Remembering that everything is interconnected helps us avoid separating and simplifying things through comparisons, dichotomies, or divisions. We can learn to patiently work against white ways of seeing (in ourselves and others) by understanding and recognizing interdependence in our daily lives. For instance, our viewpoints are interdependent. Our experiences, political views, and personal values all influence our initial interpretations of images. And the fact that reality is socially constructed means that the ways we make sense of our world (including of images) are influenced by other people and all the experiences and values that influence them in turn. Becoming aware of these connections and patterns allows us to open our minds to different perspectives.

ADDITIONAL TOOLS FOR YOUR TOOLKIT: MINDFULNESS, PLAYFULNESS, SELF-AWARENESS

We've suggested throughout this book that mindfulness can be a helpful method for challenging the lens of whiteness. We want to be mindful because we want to become aware of our assumptions. We want to be able to deal with our complex emotions around issues of whiteness, including anger. Specific mindfulness practices can help us observe our thoughts and emotions, and therefore deepen the ongoing process of unlearning white ways of seeing. We want to be able to usefully communicate with other white people on these issues, so we need to be well grounded, emotionally stable, and sensitive (but tough and resolved). So mindfulness practices will be helpful.

For all these reasons, we are going to take time here to introduce some mindfulness practices, including mindfulness meditation, which Diane has taught for years. Sitting meditation is the most foundational mindfulness practice. Like all mindfulness practices, it is a way to train our minds to pay attention to what we choose to pay attention to, rather than letting them wander randomly. It can be a religious or spiritual experience, but it need not be. It's important to remember, however, that mindfulness is deeply rooted in Eastern philosophy and religion. The discussion and instructions here draw from the Shambhala tradition based in Tibetan Buddhism. We can practice mindfulness being careful not to appropriate Eastern cultures or traditions.

Often people don't want to try meditation because they assume they have to stop their thoughts and they can't. You don't need to stop your thoughts; you learn how to work with them. Just like you could have a deep conversation with another person, or engage in meaningless chatter, our minds have a range of thoughts and emotions happening. There are also thoughts and emotions that may be difficult so they remain below our level of conscious awareness. In meditating, we clear space for some of those thoughts and emotions to come up and we also begin to see our patterns of thought. We want to have awareness of our thoughts so we can work with them. To have perspective on them, it's crucial to get some distance from the thoughts, to understand them *as* thoughts, not as something we need to believe or act on.

As you meditate, you'll notice that a single thought arises and then you create a whole storyline based on it. You may mentally comment on a hunger pang and suddenly go on a long tangent about what is in the fridge, what you need at the grocery store, whether you're spending too much on takeout, whether it's ethical to use Uber Eats, and on and on and on. As soon as you notice the storyline, you do two things. The first is to kindly label it "thinking" and let it go. Some meditators imagine the thoughts being put on a cloud and drifting away in the sky, or set on a leaf in a stream and floating away. If the thoughts don't want to go, sit with them in a friendly way. You do the same with the longest, silliest storyline or the most profound new insight (making a mental note to reflect on the profound insight after meditation!). This is because you don't judge the thoughts that come up, whether silly, profound, racist…we need to see our assumptions and judging thoughts promotes repression and guilt. Again, this doesn't mean you act on the thought or necessarily believe the thought; it also doesn't mean that judgement isn't important in other areas of our lives.

The second thing you do is return your attention to your out-breath, your posture and what is going on around you—everything that makes up the present moment. Most likely the whole process will start again with another thought, storyline, or emotion. The moment when you notice you've been thinking and return your attention to the outbreath is the moment you're actually training your attention, so don't worry about thoughts coming up.

When you meditate, sit in an upright yet relaxed posture. Silence any electronic devices, and set a timer for a short period of time, maybe five minutes (lengthen the time as you get more experience). Start by noticing each out breath as it happens. Some people choose to count each breath, starting over after reaching five or ten breaths (this is a Zen practice); others find it helpful to focus on the sensation of the breath, such as the rise and fall of the chest and belly or the feeling of the air as it exits their nostrils. Take it moment by moment, breath by breath. When you have a consistent practice, over time your mind will settle down a bit.

Mindfulness can help us become aware of our underlying assumptions, which likely have layers of subtle or overt racism, white supremacy, and a desire to be a "good white person." It helps us become aware of how our assumptions and thoughts influence how we process and interpret what we see. And the more we can consciously or mindfully observe our thoughts about an image, the more able we will be to look at it critically and with awareness of the visual conventions underlying it. In addition, it can help us observe more closely the specific features of images. It can even help us be more creative and thoughtful as we create our own images. Mindfulness can also help us be gentle with ourselves and others as we do this work, without losing accountability.

Sitting meditation is a wonderful practice that changes not only the way we see but how we act. The more we integrate it into our daily lives, the more able we'll be to handle difficult conversations and see things more critically. And what's more, once we get a sense of this practice we can adapt it to any other activity. Instead of using the breath as an anchor, come back to whatever you're doing. If you're reading (like you are right now) and notice that you've become lost in thought, bring your attention back to reading. If you're walking, same thing: don't be distracted by your phone, don't feel compelled to follow your breath; just walk. See, hear, feel what is around you. When you get lost in thought, notice and come right back to walking. You can mindfully fold the laundry, mindfully have a conversation, mindfully ride the bus.

Mindfulness meditation is just one of many mindfulness practices. Appendix C, "Additional Resources," offers some suggestions for safe space (for when things get overwhelming), loving kindness, and "just like me" practices, and these are only some of the possibilities. Apps like Headspace, Calm, and Insight Timer can provide guided meditations, support, and more in your mindfulness journey. Be discerning, as there are many teachers and practices on these apps. Look for resources that are neither trendy nor vapid and that place what they are offering in their original cultural and religious contexts, and respect their history. Attending to this is another way of undoing white ways of seeing.

Other things that will be helpful, whether or not you develop a sitting practice, are a supportive community, a sense of humor and playfulness, gentleness, resolve, and practical communication skills.

Practicing mindfulness and unlearning white ways of seeing are best done in a community of like-minded (but not too like-minded!) people who will both support and challenge us in our journey. In an article subtitled "While We Sit on Our Cushions, Systemic Racism Runs Rampant," white antiracist early childhood educator Holly Hatton-Bowers says, "I have found that real sustaining change comes from engaging in mindfulness and compassion in community and doing this alongside historical analysis."[135] We recommend that you create or join a group in which to mindfully unlearn white ways of seeing. Look for such groups in your community or online, in contemplative societies, social justice activist communities, antiracist white ally or accomplice trainings and workshops, local meditation centers, and centering prayer groups, among other places.

Playfulness and humor are ways to balance out the seriousness that goes into developing an antiracist lens. For instance, when we notice someone—including ourselves—falling into some particularly persistent assumption or interpretation, we can draw on our sense of humor and say, "Problematic assumption! Hi! There you are again!" rather than whipping up blame, shame, or guilt. The assumption arose, but we recognized it and know that we don't have to believe it, and that's a big part of the struggle. Online groups that use humor and playfulness to do serious education include No White Saviors (@nowhitesaviors) on Twitter and their podcast by the same name, the satirical charity campaign called Radi-Aid: Africa for Norway at RadiAid.com, and McSweeneys.net's satirical yet pointed articles.

America Hates Us clothing brand creates products intended to disrupt comfort levels and encourage dialogue, while also raising money for social justice causes. Or scroll through old Instagram posts of Barbie Savior (@barbiesavior) and Humanitarians of Tinder (humanitarians oftinder.com) to see comical depictions of the visual conventions we've explored.

Humor and satire can often refresh us when the work of unlearning white ways of seeing has been emotionally draining, reminding us of our shared humanity and community. We can come together to question white ways of seeing and laugh at our mistakes as we grow. It is important to share how our perspectives change, how our minds are opening to new ways of seeing. This reassures others that the process isn't effortless, that we are all works in progress when it comes to this journey.

And we will make mistakes; everyone does. It's very likely that we will see an image as unproblematic, learn something about historical contexts, microaggressions, or racial relations, and then understand we were wrong. Or we may post an image on social media and then regret it, apologize, or even remove it.

We also can't give up when someone gets defensive and attacks us for trying to speak to them about something problematic they've said or posted. Nor can we "cancel" someone when they make a mistake or aren't progressing as quickly as we'd like them to. And we can't assume that people we engage with will be combative, ignorant, or narrow-minded and that we know better than they do. In order to sustain this work throughout our lives, we will need gentleness in the form of grace and forgiveness for ourselves and for others. If we are truly attempting to unlearn our white ways of seeing, we can't shut down when someone challenges them. If we are told that something we've said or posted is racist, triggering, or inappropriate, we must be humble enough to receive the feedback and learn from it. We should also appreciate the person who expended energy and took a risk to tell us about an issue. Our humanity connects us to the person we've harmed, and we have to understand that. Getting defensive will not help. Apologizing, learning, and correcting will.

DIFFICULT CONVERSATIONS

As white people, we can no longer avoid talking about race and the role it plays in the images in our lives. If our work involves images, we need to speak up against appropriation, stereotypes, tokenism, and other racist conventions. Perhaps our company's website is problematic, or a PowerPoint presentation a colleague created has elements of white ways of seeing in it. Maybe a mockup showing people in a proposed new space or program includes no people of color, or includes them only in stereotypical clothing or roles. When we are aware of these problems, it's on us to point them out to others. This is not easy, and we need good communication skills to do it well.

The activists behind Radi-Aid, a satirical campaign asking Africans to donate radiators to relieve the plight of desperate, freezing Norwegians, along with Barbie Savior, have developed four principles to guide humanitarian volunteers who want to post images of their travels and work on social media:

1. Promote dignity
2. Gain informed consent
3. Question your intentions
4. Use your chance—Bring down stereotypes[136]

The first principle reminds us that people are not tourist attractions. Our power as white people makes us responsible for ensuring that the images we create, use, and share, and the things we write alongside them, do not harm the people in them.

The second reminds us to always ask permission to take someone's photograph, even people we know well, and to also ask permission before publicly sharing photographs in which they are identifiable. This is one way that we respect their right to privacy. Moreover, exposing the identities of people at protests and rallies, including those for social and racial justice, can place them at risk—especially with the continuing advances in facial recognition technology.

The third principle tells us to pause before we forward a meme, select a photo for our PowerPoint presentation, take a picture of someone, share a friend's post, or use images in a work project. Here are several questions to ask yourself regarding your intentions:

- Does this post primarily benefit me?
- Why am I sharing what I am sharing? Who will see this, and what am I trying to say?
- Could my message be misunderstood, and what would be the impact of that?
- Am I centering myself or exploiting others? What could I do differently?[137]

Finally, the fourth principle reminds us that we have an opportunity to change the narrative. We don't want to fall prey to the visual conventions that set up a dichotomy of "us" versus "them," tokenize people, marginalize others while centering us, or stereotype. Instead, we can shed light on the complexities and nuances of a situation and the multiple perspectives of the people involved. What story do the people in the image want to share with the world? How do we know?

Would they rather share it themselves? Do they even want to share a story at all?

These principles are meant to guide us in posting images to social media. What about when we notice our friends, family, or coworkers making mistakes due to white ways of seeing? We have to talk to them about it. Don't aggressively confront them, but start a conversation that simultaneously seeks understanding and holds people accountable.

How can we do this? Mary-Frances Winters, an author and the founder of the global diversity and inclusion consulting firm The Winters Group, writes that "bold conversations require venturing outside one's comfort zone, which can be intimidating."[138] It's important to acknowledge that it takes courage to discuss white ways of seeing. The Winters Group suggests several considerations for people preparing for such conversations.[139]

First, realize that the starting point is a place of vulnerability, for both you and the person or people you are talking with. Tell them that you are not an expert and are willing to learn. Mistakes, misunderstandings, and miscommunication will occur; acknowledge it.

Next, consider the details before beginning the conversation. Ask yourself why you are doing this, and we would add, ask yourself if you are ready to learn and be accountable. Also think about where the conversation should take place, who should be involved, and what your goal is in having it.

Third, listen actively and inclusively to others. Most of us think we are good at listening, but in reality we pay attention only to respond rather than to understand. Listening to understand requires concentrating on the other person's message and nonverbal cues. Ask open-ended questions to learn more, such as "What else concerns you about this?" or "Tell me more about that." Paraphrase what the other person communicates to clarify or confirm your understanding. Respond only when you are sure you have understood them correctly.

Next, be aware of what you are bringing to the conversation, especially your own white ways of seeing, blind spots, biases, and perspective. What you bring does matter, and, more importantly, your own awareness of what you bring is vital. The work you have done throughout this book in starting to unlearn some of your white lenses will certainly contribute to the conversation. Remember, the other person is likely to be at a different point in their journey than you, and that's okay. Honor where they are, and share where you are.

Fourth, when disagreement or conflict arises, use it as an opportunity for learning. Listen inclusively, respond without getting defensive, and find common ground. You may not change this person's ways of seeing in just a single conversation. Be prepared to have these discussions often.

Finally, continue practicing. If you get discouraged, cut yourself some slack and keep going. Communicating with others about white ways of seeing, or racism in general, is a process. It's a long journey, with bumps in the road, and you will not do it perfectly. Doing it anyway is part of the commitment you are making, and if you've made it this far in the book, we know you are ready and able to.

#WHITEWAYSOFSEEING

We invite you to keep the conversation going and continue to challenge white ways of seeing. One way to do this is to create a community of people who are exploring these issues. You can post your own reflections, analyses, and questions to social media using the #WhiteWaysOfSeeing hashtag. Together we can build on the foundation laid in this book to deconstruct the images in our everyday lives. Contribute your process, the conventions you observe, and the tropes and codes you dismantle, and call out collectively how white ways of seeing must change.

Of course, social media posts aren't going to be enough to create systemic change and eradicate white ways of seeing. To do that, we must place ourselves within the broader movement and understand that this is one part of a very long journey. As we were writing this book, the US went through a familiar cycle of racial outrage. Two years following the deaths of George Floyd, Breonna Taylor, Tony McDade, and Ahmaud Arbery, a white male teenager entered a grocery store in a Black neighborhood of Buffalo, New York, and killed ten people for explicitly racist reasons. There followed another round of white folks' awakening, public statements of commitment to justice from businesses and political leaders, some policy changes by local governments, and then a slow, quiet, exhausted retreat into "business as usual." Unlearning white ways of seeing is part of the larger fight for racial justice. Imagining a new vision for the future involves continuous engagement, regardless of how tired or overwhelmed we may feel. If you feel tired, imagine the exhaustion (and the many other things) people of color may feel.

In her book *I'm Still Here*, Austin Channing Brown describes how, in Christian communities, *justice* and *reconciliation* are apolitical buzzwords lacking a true commitment to action, equity, and change. Simply boiling reconciliation down to conversation or statistics of diversity misses the point. She suggests actions beyond dialogue, including marching in protests, supporting Black artists, and coalition building.

> When white people stop short of reconciliation, it's often because they are motivated by a deep need to believe in their own goodness, and for that goodness to be affirmed over and over and over again.

These folks want a pat on the back simply for arriving at the conclusion that having people of color around is good. But reconciliation is not about white feelings. It's about diverting power and attention to the oppressed, toward the powerless. It's not enough to dabble at diversity and inclusion while leaving the existing authority structure in place. Reconciliation demands more. Reconciliation is the pursuit of the impossible—an upside-down world where those who are powerful have relinquished that power to the margins. It's reimagining an entirely different way of being with one another. Reconciliation requires imagination. It requires looking beyond what is to what could be. It looks beyond intentions to real outcomes, real hurts, real histories.[140]

We ask you to consider how this work will impact the rest of your life. What legacy will you pass on to your friends, colleagues, kids, and grandkids? We have the power to alter the messages in the images we create and encounter every day. We can question their intention and impact. We can call out the white ways of seeing that produce and perpetuate racist, white supremacist ways of seeing. We can talk with others and learn together with our friends and family in a way that helps white people actively, compassionately dismantle our ways of perceiving and making sense of the world.

What we hope you *don't* do is put this book down after reading it and keep your insights to yourself. We also don't want you to wait until your next class, workshop, or seminar on race and whiteness to begin talking with others about white ways of seeing. Further, it should not take the murder of yet another person of color to prompt any of us to engage in antiracist activism. With intention, openness, understanding, and commitment to this lifelong work, we can all move toward antiracist ways of seeing.

ACKNOWLEDGMENTS

This book would not have been possible without the many people who helped us along the way.

Thank you to the incredible team at Skinner House—Mary Benard, Kiana Nwaobia, Larisa Hohenboken, and Pierce Alquist—and to their collaborators, Sunshine Wolfe and Shoshanna Green. It has been wonderful to work with each of you throughout the process of getting this book into the hands of readers who care. We know this book means a lot to you all as well, and we are grateful for how you carried our vision through.

We are indebted to those who read early drafts of chapters and the manuscript, giving us the gift of their time, thoughtful perspectives, critique, and feedback: Mikayla Burger, Nika Clark, Rowena Crosbie, Averi Davis, Rosalind Dean, Amanda Doyle, Kylie Fass, Danae Fuller, Hannah Hamermesh, Nicole Hanika, Abena Imhotep, Jewél Jackson, Traci Knieriem, Vivien Lee, Faith Njahira, Maya Kailani Pillsbury, Deb Rinner, Barbara Saint Aimé, Ann Scott, and Iman Wilkinson. You all challenged us, gave us incredible suggestions and ideas to consider, and enthusiastically embraced this project with us. Knowing that you all wanted and needed others to see this work gave us the courage and energy to keep going.

Thank you to the theorists, activists, scholars, meditation teachers, artists, and writers who inspired and educated us in our own white ways of seeing, including bell hooks, Patricia Hill Collins, Sara Ahmed, Eduardo Bonilla-Silva, Rachel Cargle, Brittany Cooper, Richard Dyer, Reni Eddo-Lodge, Ruth Frankenberg, Ibram X. Kendi, Zeus Leonardo, George Lipsitz, Charles W. Mills, Ijeoma Oluo, Michael Omi, Mariana Ortega, Brittany Packnett, Sally Robinson, Layla Saad, Ronald Takaki, Beverly Daniel Tatum, Patricia Williams, Howard Winant, Pema Chödrön, Ruth King, Tara Brach, Sharon Salzberg, Jack Kornfield, Jon Kabat-Zinn, Rhonda McGee, Robin Kimmerer, George Yancy, Gloria Anzaldua, Inderpal Grewal, Radha Hegde, Chandra Talpade Mohanty, Tiara Na'Puti, Raka Shome, Ngũgĩ wa Thiong'o, and Nisha Toomey.

Finally, thank you to our readers for being willing to take one step on this much longer journey with us. Let's keep traveling together.

LIZ:

Thank you to my teachers and mentors, especially Catherine Palczewski for believing in me when I didn't. To Erin Rand for making me a better writer and rhetorician. To Barbara Applebaum and Chandra Mohanty for giving me a framework to understand race and my own white privilege. To Deb Rinner and Ro Crosbie for taking a chance on me and seeing the potential in my work.

Thank you to Diane. From inception to publication, I've learned so much from you on this journey. Through laughter and tears, I wouldn't have wanted to work with anyone else. Thanks for always being there for me, book-related or not.

Thank you to friends and family who supported me in too many ways to describe here. To Mollie, Kevin, Alex, Hillari, and Mike for your constant encouragement. To Evy, Marshall, Norah, and Kerri for reminding me to stop and play, go outside, and read for fun. To Britney and Meredith, for always being a phone call away and being there whenever needed. To Annie and Mabel, for your love, support, and never-ending patience. Your encouragement that the world needed a book like this kept me afloat when the strain of writing while working full time seemed too much at times.

DIANE:

Thanks to my professors, especially Dennis Mumby. Thanks to my Syracuse writing and teaching partner Arthur Jensen and to YuLun Chou for showing me the Moesha photo shoot. To Kendall Phillips, Chuck Morris and Anne Demo for encouragement and feedback. To my single-syllable department colleagues and friends through the years: Bern Calafell, San Faulkner, Cyn Gordon, Whit Phillips, and Sylv Sierra. To Shona Hunter and Elaine Swan for inspiring me to write about worried white males, Arthur Flowers for good advice, excellent listener Jersey Cosantino, and my summer writing partner, Joan Bryant. Thank you to my research assistants, Averi Davis and Vivien Lee, who were funded through a 2020 Syracuse University SOURCE grant, for their diligence and thoroughness.

To Nina, Paris, and Harry for porch time, though only Nina could do art. To Jett for helping over many years. To the family zoom for hearing my sometimes-monologues. Thanks to my salsa friends, yoga and meditation friends, Veterans Writing Group, neighbor-friends, my god-daughter Tamika and her family, and my more-than-better half, Red, all of whom I've neglected at times while working on this book.

Finally, thank you to Liz for being the first person to walk with me on this part of the journey. We are a good team because you are so smart, so patient, and so savvy.

GLOSSARY

We use a lot of antiracist language throughout the book. While many of you may be familiar with the expressions presented here, not everyone defines them the same way. So we have compiled a list of most of the terms we use and how we define them.

Accomplice or Coconspirator: someone who proactively supports people of color, even at risk to themselves. Examples: standing alongside protestors (or behind them, or in front of them, as directed by the organizers) at Black Lives Matter rallies and marches; following the leadership of people of color in the ongoing work of changing policy, systems, beliefs, and behaviors; and not expecting to be praised for doing so.

Antiracism: opposition to racism combined with a fight for racial justice. Example: the BlackLivesMatter movement.

Ally: a term that was initially used to describe someone who participates in more marginalized people's fight for equality but that has since taken on a more pejorative meaning: those who claim to support people of color but take no meaningful action. Example: someone who claims to have participated in the Black Lives Matter movement but did nothing more than send out a couple tweets. (Note that this meaning isn't universal, as some activist groups still use "ally" positively, particularly in LGBTQ+ communities.)

BIPOC: acronym for Black people, Indigenous people, and people of color.

Calling In: challenging people's ignorance or bias by opening a compassionate dialogue with them.

Calling Out: confronting people's ignorance or bias and pointing out its unacceptability.

Cisgender, Cis: having a gender identity that matches the sex assigned at birth.

Colorblind: a term white people use when claiming we're not racist because we "don't see color." Colorblindness invalidates the experiences of people of color and implies that not being white is such a flaw that we must pretend not to notice it. Example: being confronted about racist behavior and defensively responding, "But I don't even see you as Black!"

Cultural Appropriation: using elements of another culture for one's own gain or pleasure, while the original cultural or racial group continues to be perceived and treated negatively. Example: white people with Black hairstyles such as cornrows or locs.

Gender Expression: the ways a person expresses their gender identity. Examples: name, pronouns, hair and clothing styles, vocal pitch, and choice of public bathroom.

Neocolonialism: exploitation of a former colony, and extraction of resources from it, by the former colonial power under the guise of development, humanitarianism, or capitalism.

Racial Bias: attitudes and stereotypes based on race that prompt us to perceive people of other races negatively and to act accordingly. Example: white women clutching their purses when a Black man walks past them at the mall.

Representation: the portrayal of particular groups, especially minoritized groups, in contexts from which they have typically been excluded, such as movies, politics, and business. Example: the film *Black Panther*.

Stereotype: an overly generalized idea of a type of person or thing. Not all stereotypes are negative, but even positive ones are oversimplified. Stereotypes are harmful because they narrow how people understand one another and even themselves. Examples: "Asian people are good at math"; "Black people love watermelon."

Tokenism: the inclusion of one or a few people of color, but only for symbolic and self-serving reasons. Example: a company having one Black vice president but limiting their power and influence.

White Fragility: the inability of white people to tolerate being even gently confronted with our racist thoughts, perceptions, or actions, or with the statement that we live in a racist system, and our tendency to react with defensive anger or dismissiveness. Example: "You don't know me! How can you insult me like that?"

White Guilt: white people's tendency to respond to a challenge to our racist thoughts, perceptions, or actions not by taking antiracist action but by overapologizing and becoming paralyzed by our own distress, even to the point that we expect people of color to comfort us. Example: "Oh, this is horrible . . . I had no idea . . . I can't do anything, I'm too distraught."

White Privilege: benefits white people receive in society just because we are white. Examples: having our house valued at more than it would be if we were not white; holding a barbecue in a public park without a white person calling the police; committing a traffic violation or mass shooting and being arrested unharmed. White privilege is difficult to reject because it is systemic and often invisible; we don't notice when something doesn't happen to us.

White Savior: a white person who wants to do good, help those in need, and change the world, but who is actually just maintaining racial stereotypes and power imbalances to feel good about themselves. Examples: missionaries; Peace Corps volunteers; the protagonists of movies like *Freedom Writers* and *The Blind Side*.

White Supremacy: systems and beliefs operating under the idea that the white race is superior to all other races. Such systems are not always explicitly and obviously racist, like the Ku Klux Klan and neo-Nazi organizations; white supremacy can be embedded in the everyday functioning of systems that may not appear racist on the surface. Example: the entire history of the United States.

White Tears: when white people (usually women) react to being confronted with our own racist thoughts, perceptions, or actions by crying, shutting down the conversation, centering ourselves, blaming people of color for our own reaction, and trying to solicit comfort. Example: "How can you say that about me? Nothing is enough for you people! I guess I just shouldn't talk at all then."

Woke: used positively to describe someone who is aware of and cares about issues such as racism. Used negatively to make fun of someone who is not as aware as they think they are.

FOR READING GROUPS

If you're thinking about creating a reading group for this book, we are confident you will have useful discussions. But discussions of race are fraught, so do some thinking and planning before you begin. Read guidelines for working with group dynamics; two good ones are Seal Press's guide for groups discussing Ijeoma Oluo's *So You Want to Talk about Race* (sealpress.com/wp-content/uploads/2019/04/SealPress-ReadingGuide-So-You-Want-To.pdf) and Beacon Press's guide for groups discussing Robin DiAngelo's *White Fragility* (beacon.org/assets/pdfs/whitefragilityreadingguide.pdf). Although these are intended for people working with other books, they can be useful as your group works through this one.

Consider having group members fill specific roles to support aspects of the discussion. This may include someone to start the conversation, someone to keep everyone focused on the topic, someone to monitor the time so all voices can share, and a person to play devil's advocate to call in/call out people as needed. These roles might rotate, or the people best suited to each might hold them.

And be aware of these traps that white people often fall into when discussing racial issues:

- White silence. Being silent is a privilege; make sure everyone speaks up.

- Nods that silence. A silent nod of acknowledgment stifles discussion, even if it's meant as agreement or validation. As Lynet Uttal says, "No one is listening when they have no responses. Nor does [a nod] help any of us to question our own beliefs."[141] Be ready to call out such nods and call in the people who offer nothing more than them.
- Intellectualism and theorizing. Attempts to be "objective" allow us to distance ourselves from our own white ways of seeing.
- Avoidance of our own issues. Discussions that focus on people of color rather than our own beliefs, behaviors, and white ways of seeing are not engaging with the problem.
- Self-protectiveness. Telling stories about our interactions with people of color to prove we are antiracist, and judging or putting down other white people for not being progressive enough, are attempts to make ourselves look better. We must strive to be better, not just look better.

Also recognize that one critique of book clubs is that they make white people feel good, but they don't actually make any difference.[142] Therefore, we suggest your reading group go beyond discussing your own white ways of seeing to take action together. Ibram X. Kendi, author of *How to Be an Antiracist*, suggests book clubs should "use a session or two after reading a particular book to decide as a group or individuals how they are going to directly apply what they've learned to their lives."[143] Some groups use a three-part structure for their discussions; they want to engage head, heart, and hands. Once your group has gelled, think about how you can work toward systemic change, being led and learning from people and organizations of color, and especially from Black activists.

How your group conducts itself will also be greatly affected by the racial and ethnic identities of its members. For mixed-race groups, we recommend having coleaders from different racial identity groups and caucusing by identity. This means that you break into same-race identity groups for part of the discussion. If you invite people of color to facilitate and educate your group, consider paying them for their labor and knowledge.

If your group is entirely white, consider bringing in people of color as leaders and guest experts. Pay them for their labor and knowledge. We also recommend asking each member to do some self-reflective antiracism work before joining the reading group. Possibilities include completing Layla Saad's workbook *Me and White Supremacy;* participating in Rachel Cargle's The Great Unlearn, an online learning collective, or completing her "Do the Work" course; and taking a workshop through Equity in the Center (equityinthecenter.org). You can find these in appendix C, "Additional Resources," and of course there are many more.[144]

Though we're not experts on reading groups, we do have some relevant skills and we'd be happy to talk with people thinking of starting one.

APPENDIX C

ADDITIONAL RESOURCES

Books and Articles

Emmanuel Acho, *Uncomfortable Conversations with a Black Man*, 2020

Michelle Alexander, *The New Jim Crow: Mass Incarceration in the Age of Colorblindness*, 10th anniversary edition, 2020

Carol Anderson, *White Rage*, 2017

James Baldwin, "Stranger in the Village," *Harper's Magazine*, October 1953

Roland Barthes, *Camera Lucida: Reflections on Photography*, 1980

Jacqueline Battalora, *Birth of a White Nation: The Invention of White People and Its Relevance Today*, 2013

John Berger, *Ways of Seeing*, 1990

Maurice Berger, *Whiteness and Race in Contemporary Art*, 2004

Kahran Bethencourt and Regis Bethencourt, *Glory: Magical Visions of Black Beauty*, 2020 (and the website of their business, CreativeSoul Photography, creativesoulphoto.com)

Daniel C. Blight, ed., *The Image of Whiteness: Contemporary Photography and Racialization*, 2019

Eduardo Bonilla-Silva, *Racism without Racists: Color-Blind Racism and the Persistence of Racial Inequality in America*, 6th edition, 2021

Austin Channing Brown, *I'm Still Here: Black Dignity in a World Made for Whiteness*, 2018

Ta-Nehisi Coates, *Between the World and Me*, 2015

Teju Cole, "The White-Savior Industrial Complex," *The Atlantic*, March 2012

Anthony Cortese, *Provocateur: Images of Women and Minorities in Advertising*, 1999

Kimberlé Williams Crenshaw, Luke Charles Harris, Daniel Martinez HoSang, and George Lipsitz, *Seeing Race Again: Countering Colorblindness across the Disciplines*, 2019

Angela Davis and Frank Barat, *Freedom Is a Constant Struggle: Ferguson, Palestine, and the Foundations of a Movement*, 2016

Reni Eddo-Lodge, *Why I'm No Longer Talking to White People about Race*, 2017

Christopher Emdin, *For White Folks Who Teach in the Hood—and the Rest of Y'all Too: Reality Pedagogy and Urban Education*, 2017

Janette Faulkner, Robbin Henderson, Pamela Fabry, and Adam David Miller, *Ethnic Notions: Black Images in the White Mind; An Exhibition of Afro-American Stereotype and Caricature from the Collection of Janette Faulkner*, exhibition catalogue, Berkeley Art Center, 1982

Paula Giddings, *When and Where I Enter: The Impact of Black Women on Race and Sex in America*, 1984

Nikole Hannah-Jones, *The 1619 Project: A New Origin Story*, 2021

Cheryl Harris, "Whiteness as Property," in *Black on White: Black Writers on What It Means to Be White*, ed. David Roediger, 103–17, 1999

myisha t hill, *Heal Your Way Forward: The Co-Conspirator's Guide to an Antiracist Future*, 2022

Patricia Hill Collins, "Mammies, Matriarchs, and Other Controlling Images," chapter 4 in *Black Feminist Thought: Knowledge, Consciousness and the Politics of Empowerment*, 1991

bell hooks, *Black Looks: Race and Representation*, 1992

Harriet Jacobs, *Incidents in the Life of a Slave Girl, Written by Herself*, 1987

George Lipsitz, *The Possessive Investment in Whiteness: How White People Profit from Identity Politics*, 1998

James Loewen, *Lies My Teacher Told Me: Everything Your American History Textbook Got Wrong*, 1996

Ijeoma Oluo, *Mediocre: The Dangerous Legacy of White Male America*, 2020

Jan Nederveen Pieterse, *White on Black: Images of Africa and Blacks in Western Popular Culture*, 1992

Rosetta Quisenberry, *A Saga of the Black Woman*, 2003 (and the others in the series: *The Black Man, The Black Child*, and *The Black Family*)

Sally Robinson, *Marked Men: White Masculinity in Crisis*, 2000

Layla F. Saad, *Me and White Supremacy: Combat Racism, Change the World, and Become a Good Ancestor*, 2020

Jonathan Schroeder, *Visual Consumption*, 2002

Raka Shome, *Diana and Beyond: White Femininity, National Identity, and Contemporary Media Culture*, 2014

Susan Sontag, *On Photography*, 1979

Susan Sontag, *Regarding the Pain of Others*, 2003

Ronald Takaki, *Iron Cages: Race and Culture in 19th-Century America*, 1990

Beverly Daniel Tatum, *Why Are All the Black Kids Sitting Together in the Cafeteria? And Other Conversations about Race*, 20th anniversary edition, 2017

Keeanga-Yamahtta Taylor, *From #BlackLivesMatter to Black Liberation*, 2016

Alok Vaid-Menon, *Beyond the Gender Binary*, 2020

Veronica T. Watson, *The Souls of White Folk: African American Writers Theorize Whiteness*, 2013

Ida B. Wells-Barnett, *A Red Record*, 1895

George Yancy, *Black Bodies, White Gazes: The Continuing Significance of Race*, 2008

Podcasts and Videos

1619, hosted by Nikole Hannah-Jones, produced by the *New York Times*

About Race, hosted by Reni-Eddo Lodge

The Art of Manliness hosted by Brett McKay

Code Switch, produced by National Public Radio

The Cut, produced by Vox Media Podcast Network

DFW (Divesting from Whiteness), hosted by Joquina Reed

Intersectionality Matters, by Kimberlé Crenshaw

Las Doctoras, hosted by Dr. Renee Lemus and Dr. Cristina Rose

Man Up, hosted by Aymann Ismail, produced by *Slate*

Nice White Parents, hosted by Chana Joffe-Walt, produced by the *New York Times*

Our Body Politic, hosted by Farai Chideya, produced by Diaspora Farms

Pod Save the People, hosted by DeRay Mckesson, produced by Crooked Media

Popaganda, hosted by Carmen Rios, produced by Bitch Media

Silence Is Not an Option, hosted by Don Lemon

Seeing White, hosted by John Biewen, produced by Scene on Radio

Unladylike, hosted by Cristen Conger

The White Saviors, hosted by Olusola Adeogun, produced by Canadaland

Whiteness at Work, produced by Media & Entertainment Podcasts

Yo, Is This Racist? hosted by Andrew Ti and Tawny Newsome

Larry Adelman, producer, *Race: The Power of an Illusion*, California Newsreel, 2003

Jacqueline Battalora, "Birth of a White Nation," video of speech, youtube.com/watch?v=riVAuC0dnP4, 2014

Courses

Equity in the Center, "Intersectional Allyship for Racial Justice: A Workshop for White Allies" https://equityinthecenter.org/services/culture-trainings/intersectional-allyship-for-white-allies/

Rachel Cargle, "Do the Work," a free thirty-day course "designed to be an eye-opener and a call to action for those who seek to be allies to Black women," mailchi.mp/rachelcargle/dothework-course-all-30days.

Rachel Cargle, The Great Unlearn, an online, self-paced, self-priced learning collective, rachelcargle.com/the-great-unlearn/.

MINDFULNESS RESOURCES
Books

Beth Berila, *Integrating Mindfulness into Anti-oppression Pedagogy*, 2016

Pema Chödrön, *The Wisdom of No Escape and the Path of Loving-Kindness*, 1991

Ruth King, *Mindful of Race: Transforming Race from the Inside Out*, 2018

Rhonda Magee, *The Inner Work of Racial Justice: Healing Ourselves and Transforming Our Communities through Mindfulness*, 2019

Thích Nhất Hạnh, *The Sun My Heart: From Mindfulness to Insight Contemplation*, 1988

Lama Rod Owens, *Love and Rage: The Path of Liberation through Anger*, 2020

Chade-Meng Tan, *Search Inside Yourself: The Unexpected Path to Achieving Success, Happiness (and World Peace)*, 2014

Rev. angel Kyodo williams and Lama Rod Owens, with Jasmine Syedullah, *Radical Dharma: Talking Race, Love, and Liberation*, 2017

Podcasts

Metta Hour, hosted by Sharon Salzberg, produced by the Be Here Now Network

Tara Brach, hosted by Tara Brach

Tricycle Talks, produced by *Tricycle: The Buddhist Review*

Organizations

The Association for the Contemplative Mind in Higher Education

The Center for Compassion and Altruism Research and Education

The Garrison Institute

The Greater Good Science Center

The Mind & Life Institute

Practices

If you are under the care of a doctor, therapist, or other caregiver, you may want to let them know about your practice and get support if needed. If you would like to listen to these instructions as you practice, you can record yourself reading them or look for audio versions online. In addition to the mindfulness meditation practice described in chapter 6, you will find additional instructions for other mindfulness practices below.

Safe Space Practice

It's wise to create a safe space practice for yourself. Think of a real or imaginary place where you feel wonderful—safe and loved. Imagine it in detail. What do you see, hear, smell, taste, feel around you? What do you experience as you move through this space? Make the experience as rich and detailed as possible. In your sitting practice, if you ever start to feel very uncomfortable, or if thoughts or feelings arise that you are not ready to deal with, you can choose to go into a safe space practice rather than stopping the meditation altogether. If you are struggling, speak with a trusted meditation teacher.

A loving-kindness meditation

May I be happy

May I be healthy

May I be free from pain and suffering

May all beings be happy

May all beings be healthy

May all beings be free from pain and suffering

Just like Me Practice

Take an upright yet relaxed position. Take a minute to follow your out breath. Then imagine someone you know: perhaps someone you care about, or perhaps someone with whom you feel tension (or both!). Now slowly read (or listen to a recording of) the text below.

> This person has a body and a mind, just like me.
> This person has feelings, thoughts, and emotions, just like me.
> This person has, at some point in their life, been sad, disappointed, angry, hurt, or confused, just like me.
> This person has, in their life, experienced physical and emotional pain and suffering, just like me.
> This person wishes to be free from pain and suffering, just like me.
> This person wishes to be healthy and loved, and to have fulfilling relationships, just like me.
> This person wishes to be happy, just like me.
>
> I wish for this person to have the strength, the resources, and the emotional and social support they need to navigate the difficulties in life.
> I wish for this person to be free from pain and suffering.
> I wish for this person to be happy.
> Because this person is a fellow human being, just like me.
>
> Now I wish for all beings to be happy.

Take a minute to follow your out breath again.

(This practice is based on one in Chade-Meng Tan's book *Search Inside Yourself: The Unexpected Path to Achieving Success, Happiness (and World Peace)*. You may find it a bit perplexing; does it mean we don't wish a person those good things if they aren't like us (or if we don't see them as being like us)? However, people who follow this practice while thinking of someone they're in tension with often do find that their feelings toward the person shift, so we include it here.)

ENDNOTES

1 See Thomas Kochman, *Black and White Styles in Conflict*, pp 89–91 (Chicago: University of Chicago Press, 1981).

2 Screenshots of Dove advertisement, 2017, taken from Casey Quackenbush, "Dove Apologizes after Body Wash Ad Is Slammed for Being Racist," time.com/4974075/dove-apology-racist-ad. See also a Fairy Soap ad in Will Heilpern, "18 Awful Vintage Ads from the 20th Century That Show How Far We Have Progressed," *Insider*, April 17, 2016, businessinsider.com/vintage-sexist-and-racist-ads-2016-4; Lautz Bro's & Co's Stearine Soap ad, in Livia Gershon, "The Racism of 19th-Century Advertisements," *JSTOR Daily*, January 28, 2019, daily. jstor.org/the-racism-of-19th-century-advertisements/; a Pears' Soap ad, 1884, in Hong Wrong, "A Centuries-Old 'Joke': Racist Chinese Detergent Ad a Rip-Off of Italian Commercial," *Hong Kong Free Press*, March 31, 2020, hongkongfp.com/2016/05/27/a-century-old -joke-racist-chinese-detergent-ad-a-rip-off-of-italian-commercial.

3 Dove (@Dove), "An image we recently posted on Facebook missed the mark in representing women of color thoughtfully. We deeply regret the offense it caused," Twitter, October 7, 2017, twitter.com/dove/ status/916731793927278592.

4 Estelle Shirbon, "Dove Faces PR Disaster over Ad That Showed Black Woman Turning White," *Reuters*, October 9, 2017, reuters.com/ article/us-unilever-dove-advert/dove-faces-pr-disaster-over-ad-that -showed-black-woman-turning-white-idUSKBN1CE17M.

5 Lisa Wade, "Doctoring Diversity: Race and Photoshop," Sociological Images, *The Society Pages*, September 2, 2009, thesocietypages.org/ socimages/2009/09/02/doctoring-diversity-race-and-photoshop/.

6 Scott Jaschik, "York College of Pennsylvania Illustrates the Issues When Colleges Change Photographs to Project Diversity," *Inside Higher Ed*, February 4, 2019, insidehighered.com/admissions/article/ 2019/02/04/york-college-pennsylvania-illustrates-issues-when -colleges-change.

7 Kimberly J. Norwood, "'If You Is White, You's Alright. . . .': Stories about Colorism in America," *Washington University Global Studies Law Review* 14, no. 4 (2015), openscholarship.wustl.edu/cgi/view content.cgi?article=1547&context=law_globalstudies.

8 "Project #ShowUs," Dove, accessed October 10, 2021, dove.com/us/en/stories/campaigns/showus.html.

9 Shereena Farrington, "A Case Study on Black Twitter's Reactions to the Framing of Blacks in Dove's 2017 Facebook Advertisement," master's thesis, University of South Florida, 2020, accessed October 10, 2021, digitalcommons.usf.edu/cgi/viewcontent.cgi?article=9643 &context=etd, 43.

10 Nicholas Sammond, *Birth of an Industry: Blackface Minstrelsy and the Rise of American Animation* (Durham, NC: Duke University Press, 2015).

11 bell hooks, *Yearning: Race, Gender, and Cultural Politics* (Boston: South End Press, 1990), 54; bell hooks, *Black Looks: Race and Representation* (Boston: South End Press, 1992).

12 Jacqueline Battalora, *Birth of a White Nation: The Invention of White People and Its Relevance Today* (New York: Routledge, 2013).

13 Michelle Alexander, *The New Jim Crow: Mass Incarceration in the Age of Colorblindness*, revised edition (New York: New Press, 2012); Isabel Wilkerson, *Caste: The Origins of Our Discontents* (New York: Random House, 2020).

14 V. Jean Ramsey, "A Different Way of Making a Difference: Learning through Feelings," *Journal of Organizational Change Management* 7, no. 6 (1994): 59–71.

15 Peggy McIntosh, "White Privilege and Male Privilege: A Personal Account of Coming to See Correspondences through Work in Women's Studies," in *Race, Class and Gender: An Anthology*, ed. Margaret Anderson and Patricia Hill Collins, 3rd ed. (Belmont, CA: Wadsworth, 1998), 94–105.

16 Layla F. Saad, *Me and White Supremacy: Combat Racism, Change the World, and Become a Good Ancestor* (Naperville, IL: Sourcebooks, 2020), 14.

17 Thank you to Barbara Saint Aimé for this insight.

18 Austin Channing Brown, *I'm Still Here: Black Dignity in a World Made for Whiteness* (New York: Convergent Books, 2018), 104.

19 Andrew Holecek, "The Lost Art of Contemplation," *Tricycle: The Buddhist Review*, February 1, 2021, tricycle.org/magazine/buddhist -contemplation/.

20 Thank you to Abena Imhotep for this insight.

21 George Yancy, "Whiteness: 'Unseen' Things Seen," in *Black Bodies, White Gazes: The Continuing Significance of Race* (Lanham, MD: Rowman and Littlefield, 2008), 33–64.

22 "Education," Project Implicit, accessed August 1, 2019, implicit.harvard.edu/implicit/education.html.

23 Jan Nederveen Pieterse, *White on Black: Images of Africa and Blacks in Western Popular Culture* (New Haven: Yale University Press, 1992), 207.

24 This section is partially based on Arthur Jensen, Barnett Pearce, and Diane Grimes, "The Art of Making Better Social Worlds: Communication as a Social Force" (unpublished manuscript, in the authors' possession, 2003).

25 Peter Berger and Thomas Luckmann, *The Social Construction of Reality* (Harlow, England: Penguin Books, 1991).

26 Kenneth Burke, *Permanence and Change* (New York: New Republic, 1935), 49.

27 "Six/Nine: Matter of Perspective Cartoon," Lens Shift, September 18, 2018, lensshift.org/library/six-nine-matter-of-perspective-cartoon.

28 Patricia Hill Collins, *Black Feminist Thought: Knowledge, Consciousness, and the Politics of Empowerment* (New York: Routledge, 1991); Sandra Harding, *Whose Science/Whose Knowledge?* (Ithaca, NY: Cornell University Press, 1991).

29 Tambay Obenson, "Demand for Reproduced Racist Memorabilia Grows Worldwide—A New Doc Investigates," *IndieWire*, February 4, 2019, indiewire.com/2019/02/racist-memorabilia-market-blackface-demand-1202040313.

30 Kimberlé Crenshaw, "Mapping the Margins: Intersectionality, Identity Politics, and Violence against Women of Color," *Stanford Law Review* 43, no. 6 (1991): 1241–99.

31 Jon Simpson, "Finding Brand Success in the Digital World," Forbes Agency Council, August 25, 2017, forbes.com/sites/forbesagencycouncil/2017/08/25/finding-brand-success-in-the-digital-world.

32 John Berger, *Ways of Seeing: Based on the BBC Television Series with John Berger* (London: British Broadcasting Corporation and Penguin Books, 1990).

33 W. J. T. Mitchell, "Showing Seeing: A Critique of Visual Culture," *Journal of Visual Culture* 1, no. 2 (August 2002): 170–71, doi.org/10.1177/147041290200100202.

34 Janet Borgerson and Jonathan Schroeder, "Ethical Issues of Global Marketing: Avoiding Bad Faith in Visual Representation," *European Journal of Marketing* 36, nos. 5–6 (2002): 579.

35 "Tropical Punch," *Teen Vogue*, May 2005, 136–41. The discussions of the photoshoots of Moesha, the day at the beach, and Mona in this chapter draw on Diane Grimes and YuLun Chou, "Juicy Fruit Charms: Race, Bodies, and Representation in *Teen Vogue* Magazine" (paper presented at the annual convention of the National Communication Association, Chicago, November 2007).

36 Pieterse, *White on Black*, 199.

37 Jonathan Schroeder, *Visual Consumption* (New York: Routledge, 2002), 29.

38 Borgerson and Schroeder, "Ethical Issues of Global Marketing," 583.

39 Jane Desmond, *Staging Tourism: Bodies on Display from Waikiki to Sea World* (Chicago: University of Chicago Press, 1999).

40 Noah Dolim, "Misperceptions of the 'Hula Girl,'" *Hohonu: A Journal of Academic Writing* 12 (2014): 1–5, hilo.hawaii.edu/campuscenter/hohonu/volumes/documents/MisperceptionsoftheHulaGirlNoahDolim.pdf.

41 Dolim, "Misperceptions," 3.

42 Julie Kaomea, "A Curriculum of Aloha? Colonialism and Tourism in Hawai'i's Elementary Textbooks," *Curriculum Inquiry* 30, no. 3 (Autumn 2000): 319–44.

43 Comment by Erin Kerrison in Kerrison, Wizdom Powell, and Abigail Sewell, "Object to Subject: Three Scholars on Race, Othering, and Bearing Witness," interview by Andrew Grant-Thomas, *Othering & Belonging* 3 (2018), otheringandbelonging.org/object-subject-three-scholars-race-othering-bearing-witness.

44 Robert Miles, *Racism* (London: Routledge, 1989); Ronald Takaki, *Iron Cages: Race and Culture in 19th-Century America* (New York: Oxford University Press, 1990).

45 hooks, *Black Looks*, 21, 39.

46 hooks, *Black Looks*, 72.

47 Mous Lamrabat et al., "Bright Ideas," *Vogue*, March 2021, 210–13.

48 Clive Dexter, "Posing Secrets for the Legs and Feet," Ezbackgrounds, accessed May 30, 2021, ezbackgrounds.com/blog/how-to-pose-legs-feet.php.

49 Anthony Cortese, *Provocateur: Images of Women and Minorities in Advertising* (New York: Rowman and Littlefield, 1999), 143.

50 Cortese, *Provocateur*, 143–44.

51 Joel Anderson, Elise Holland, Courtney Heldreth, and Scott P. Johnson, "Revisiting the Jezebel Stereotype: The Impact of Target Race on Sexual Objectification," *Psychology of Women Quarterly* 42, no. 4 (December 1, 2018): 461–76, doi.org/10.1177/0361684318791543.

52 Lydie Moudileno, "Returning Remains: Saartjie Baartman, or the 'Hottentot Venus' as Transnational Postcolonial Icon," *Modern Language Studies* 45, no. 2 (April 2009): 200–212.

53 Jason Chambers, "Taste Matters: Bikinis, Twins, and Catfights in Sexually Oriented Beer Advertising," *Sex in Consumer Culture: The Erotic Content of Media and Marketing*, ed. Tom Reichert and Jacqueline Lambiase (New York: Lawrence Erlbaum, 2006), 162.

54 hooks, *Black Looks*, 73.

55 Hill Collins, *Black Feminist Thought*, 77–78.

56 Joanna Schlenzka and Myro Wulff, "Elle Style: What to Wear & How to Wear It," *Elle UK*, March 2021, 71–77.

57 "Wm. H. West's Big Minstrel Jubilee," image of 1900 advertising poster, Wikipedia, s.v. "Blackface," accessed May 31, 2021, en.wikipedia .org/wiki/Blackface#/media/File:Minstrel_PosterBillyVanWare_edit .jpg.

58 Kekla Magoon, "Our Modern Minstrelsy," *The Horn Book*, June 17, 2020, hbook.com/?detailStory=our-modern-minstrelsy.

59 Julia Craven, "Here's a Reminder Not to Wear Blackface This Halloween (or Ever)," *Huffington Post*, October 30, 2015, updated November 1, 2016, huffpost.com/entry/dont-wear-blackface-halloween_n_5633 b4dde4b06317991244ac.

60 Magoon, "Modern Minstrelsy."

61 Rosetta Lucas Quisenberry, *A Saga of the Black Woman* (self-published, 2003), 45.

62 Janette Faulkner, Robbin Henderson, Pamela Fabry, and Adam David Miller, *Ethnic Notions: Black Images in the White Mind; An Exhibition of Afro-American Stereotype and Caricature from the Collection of Janette Faulkner*, exhibition catalogue, Berkeley Art Center, 1982, 90.

63 Hill Collins, *Black Feminist Thought*, 70–73.

64 Quisenberry, *Saga of the Black Woman*.

65 "Making Waves," *Teen Vogue*, May 2005, 168–73.

66 "One Word: Plastics," *Teen Vogue*, February 2005, 144–49.

67 "About Us," CreativeSoul Photography, accessed May 25, 2021, creativesoulphoto.com/about/.

68 "AfroArt Series," CreativeSoul Photography, accessed August 27, 2022, creativesoulphoto.com/afroart-series/.

69 Alisha Acquaye, "CreativeSoul AfroArt Photo Series Highlights Natural Hair," *Teen Vogue*, February 20, 2018, teenvogue.com/gallery/ creativesoul-afroart-photo-series-highlights-natural-hair.

70 Bianca Betancourt, "Jari Jones's Calvin Klein Campaign Was a Moment of Manifestation," *Harper's Bazaar*, July 10, 2020, harpers

bazaar.com/culture/features/a33265266/jari-jones-calvin-klein
-campaign-interview/.

71 Jari Jones, "Cut the Wings: Trans Model and Activist Jari Jones Takes
on Victoria's Secret's Blatant Lack of Inclusion," *Essence*, updated
October 23, 2020, essence.com/fashion/cut-the-wings-victorias-secret
-fashion-show-2018/.

72 Jari Jones, @IamJariJones, *Twitter*, June 19, 2020, https://twitter.com/
IAmJariJones/status/1274028930626924546

73 Yahoo Life Beth Greenfield Jari Jones, face of Calvin Klein's Pride campaign, celebrates massive billboard: 'a Fat Black Trans Woman Looks
over New York' June 26, 2020 https://www.yahoo.com/video/jari-jones
-face-calvin-klein-pride-campaign-celebrates-massive-billboard
-221054617.html

74 "Jari Jones on Visibility, Nurturing Her Community, and Her Multi-
faceted Career," interview by Kimberly Drew, *Teen Vogue*, September
9, 2020, teenvogue.com/story/jari-jones-cover-september-2020.

75 Quil Lemons, "About," accessed October 10, 2021, quillemons.com/
ABOUT.

76 See, for instance, Karen E. Carr, "Medieval African History—Timbuktu and Great Zimbabwe," Quatr.us, accessed October 3, 2017,
quatr.us/african-history/medieval-african-history-timbuktu-great
-zimbabwe.htm; ABS Contributor, "7 Medieval African Kingdoms
Everyone Should Know About," *Atlanta Black Star*, December 5, 2013,
atlantablackstar.com/2013/12/05/7-midieval-african-kingdoms/;
George E. Brooks, "African 'Landlords' and European 'Strangers':
African–European Relations to 1870," in *Africa*, 2nd ed., ed. Phyllis
Martin and Patrick O'Meara (Bloomington: Indiana University Press,
1986), 104–21; Pieterse, *White on Black*.

77 Pieterse, *White on Black*, 29.

78 Sheldon Gellar, "The Colonial Era," in *Africa*, 2nd ed., ed. Phyllis
Martin and Patrick O'Meara (Bloomington: Indiana University Press,
1986), 122–40.

79 Pieterse, *White on Black*, 30–31.

80 "Hominids," Strange Science, accessed September 3, 2021, strange
science.net/sthom1.htm.

81 Sibly, E. (1795). *An Universal System of Natural History: Including
the Natural History of Man, the Orang-Outang and the Whole Tribe
of Simia*. Volume Two. London: Printed for the Proprietor: Sold by
Champante.

82 Pieterse, *White on Black*, 38.

83 Todd Wright, "'Lil' Monkey' Doll Brings Racism to the Toy Aisle," NBC Miami, August 13, 2009, nbcmiami.com/news/local/lil-monkey-doll-no-longer-at-a-costco-near-you/1837609/.

84 Liam Stack, "H&M Apologizes for 'Monkey' Image Featuring Black Child," *New York Times*, January 8, 2018, nytimes.com/2018/01/08/business/hm-monkey.html.

85 "Christopher Columbus Monument," Syracuse Then and Now, accessed September 5, 2021, syracusethenandnow.org/Dwntwn/Columbus/ColumbusStatue/ColumbusStatue.htm (site discontinued).

86 Though we prefer the term *Indigenous*, we use *Native American* here for consistency with those we are quoting.

87 James Loewen, *Lies across America: What Our Historic Sites Get Wrong* (New York: Simon and Schuster, 1999), 16.

88 "Christopher Columbus Monument."

89 Mary Whittington, "Critical Opinion on the Columbus Monument of Syracuse, New York," August 8, 2021 (Syracuse, NY: Syracuse Peace Council, Neighbors of the Onondaga), in authors' possession.

90 "Pin by Bryon Thompson on Haudenosaunee: Feather Headdress, Mohawk Indians, Iroquois." Pinterest, March 9, 2018, pinterest.com/pin/88946161375892069/; "Dress," Onondaga Nation, January 27, 2021, onondaganation.org/culture/dress/.

91 Whittington, "Critical Opinion."

92 "Christopher Columbus," Wikiquote, accessed September 5, 2021, en.wikiquote.org/wiki/Christopher_Columbus.

93 Mark Roosevelt, "Theodore Roosevelt's Great-Grandson Says: Remove the Statue," CBS News, July 12, 2020, cbsnews.com/news/theodore-roosevelts-great-grandson-mark-roosevelt-says-remove-the-statue/.

94 Michael Galen and A. Palmer, "White, Male, and Worried," *Business Week*, January 31, 1994, 50–54.

95 Renee Blank and Sandra Slipp, "The White Male: An Endangered Species?" *Management Review*, September 1994, 27–32.

96 Tiffany Burns, Jess Huang, Alexis Krivkovich, Ishanaa Rambachan, Tijana Trkulja, and Lareina Yee, "Women in the Workplace 2021," McKinsey and Company, accessed September 27, 2021, mckinsey.com/featured-insights/diversity-and-inclusion/women-in-the-workplace.

97 Schroeder, *Visual Consumption*, 103.

98 Schroeder, *Visual Consumption*, 100.

99 Robyn Morris, "Reading Photographically: Translating Whiteness through the Eye of the Empire," *Hecate; St. Lucia* 27, no. 2 (October 2001): 90.

100 Scott Ferry, "A Point of View: Confronting White Fragility and Male Fragility with Empathy," The Inclusion Solution, March 26, 2020, theinclusionsolution.me/confronting-white-fragility-and-male-fragility -with-empathy/.

101 Sonia Thompson, "Should You Ask Diverse Members of Your Team to Help Attract More Diverse Talent?," *Inc.*, October 30, 2020, inc.com/ sonia-thompson/should-you-ask-diverse-members-of-your-team-to -help-attract-more-diverse-talent.html.

102 Charlene M. Solomon, "Are White Males Being Left Out?," *Personnel Journal*, November 1991, 88.

103 Diane Grimes, "Challenging the Status Quo? Whiteness in the Diversity Management Literature," *Management Communication Quarterly* 15, no. 3 (February 2002): 381–409, doi.org/10.1177/0893318902153003.

104 Solomon, "White Males," 91.

105 Michael Galen and A. Palmer, "White, Male, and Worried," *Business Week*, January 31, 1994, 50–54.

106 Takaki, *Iron Cages*, 13.

107 Schroeder, *Visual Consumption*, 96.

108 Galen and Palmer, "White, Male, and Worried," 50.

109 Emily Peck, "These 8 Men Have as Much Money as Half the World," *Huffington Post*, January 15, 2017, updated January 16, huffpost.com/ entry/income-inequality-oxfam_n_58792e6ee4b0b3c7a7b13616.

110 Thank you to our copyeditor Shoshanna Green for this insight.

111 Lily Zheng, "How to Show White Men That Diversity and Inclusion Efforts Need Them," *Harvard Business Review*, October 28, 2019, hbr. org/2019/10/how-to-show-white-men-that-diversity-and-inclusion -efforts-need-them.

112 Teju Cole, "The White-Savior Industrial Complex," *The Atlantic*, March 21, 2012, theatlantic.com/international/archive/2012/03/ the-white-savior-industrial-complex/254843/.

113 Cole, "White-Savior Industrial Complex."

114 Saad, *Me and White Supremacy*, 136.

115 "Research and Statistics," Short Term Missions, accessed October 10, 2021, shorttermmissions.com/articles/mission-trip-research.

116 "Short-Term Mission Trips: Are They Worth the Investment?," Baylor University Media & Public Relations, May 2, 2011, baylor.edu/media communications/news.php?action=story&story=93238.

117 Saad, *Me and White Supremacy*, 136.

118 Kelly J. Madison, "Legitimation Crisis and Containment: The 'Anti-racist White Hero' Film," *Critical Studies in Mass Communication* 16, no. 4 (December 1999): 399–416.

119 Madison, "Legitimation Crisis," 414.

120 Ijeoma Oluo, *So You Want to Talk about Race* (New York: Seal Press, 2019), 146.

121 Sara Ahmed, *Strange Encounters: Embodied Others in Post-coloniality* (New York: Routledge, 2000), 116.

122 Ahmed, *Strange Encounters*, 117 (emphasis in original).

123 Sean P. Smith, "Instagram Abroad: Performance, Consumption and Colonial Narrative in Tourism," *Postcolonial Studies* 21, no. 2 (2018): 183.

124 Smith, "Instagram Abroad," 172.

125 Jon Feinstein, "What Does It Mean to Photograph Someone from Behind?," Humble Arts Foundation, May 10, 2016, hafny.org/blog/2016/5/what-does-it-mean-to-photograph-someone-from-behind.

126 Jim Richardson, "The View from the Back," *National Geographic*, accessed March 17, 2019, nationalgeographic.com/photography/article/view-from-the-back-richardson.

127 Smith, "Instagram Abroad," 180.

128 Smith, "Instagram Abroad," 180.

129 Smith, "Instagram Abroad," 177.

130 Yancy, *Black Bodies, White Gazes*, 3.

131 Susan Sontag, *Regarding the Pain of Others* (New York: Picador, 2003), 66.

132 Ariella Azoulay, *The Civil Contract of Photography* (New York: Zone Books, 2008), 130.

133 Audre Lorde, "The Uses of Anger," *Women's Studies Quarterly: Looking Back, Moving Forward* 25, nos. 1–2 (Spring–Summer 1997): 283.

134 Rachel Alicia Griffin, "I AM an Angry Black Woman: Black Feminist Autoethnography, Voice, and Resistance," *Women's Studies in Communication* 35, no. 2 (January 2012): 148, doi.org/10.1080/0749140 9.2012.724524.

135 Michael Yellow Bird, Maria Gehl, Holly Hatton-Bowers, Laurel M. Hicks, and Debbie Reno-Smith, "PERSPECTIVES—Defunding Mindfulness: While We Sit on Our Cushions, Systemic Racism Runs Rampant," *Zero to Three*, October 30, 2020, zerotothree.org/resources/3715-perspectives-defunding-mindfulness-while-we-sit-on-our-cushions-systemic-racism-runs-rampant.

136 "The Social Media Guide," Radi-Aid, accessed October 10, 2021, radiaid.com/social-media-guide.

137 Adapted from "Question Your Intentions," Radi-Aid, accessed October 10, 2021, radiaid.com/question-your-intentions.

138 Mary Frances Winters, *We Can't Talk about That at Work! How to Talk about Race, Religion, Politics, and Other Polarizing Topics* (Oakland: Berrett-Koehler Publishers, 2017), 30.

139 "Bold, Inclusive Conversations: Addressing Race & Racism in the Workplace," The Winters Group, 2018, accessed July 2, 2022, winters group.com/wp-content/uploads/2019/07/Addressing-Race-and -Racism-in-the-Workplace.pdf, 9.

140 Brown, *I'm Still Here*, 171–72.

141 Lynet Uttal, "Nods that Silence," in *Making Face, Making Soul = Haciendo Caras: Creative and Critical Perspectives by Feminists of Color*, ed. Gloria Anzaldúa (San Francisco: Aunt Lute Books, 1990), biblioteca -alternativa.noblogs.org/files/2010/09/nods_that_silence.pdf.

142 Tre Johnson, "When Black People Are in Pain, White People Just Join Book Clubs," *Washington Post*, June 11, 2020, washingtonpost.com/ outlook/white-antiracist-allyship-book-clubs/2020/06/11/9edcc766 -abf5-11ea-94d2-d7bc43b26bf9_story.html.

143 Fabiola Cineas, "The Lofty Goals and Short Life of the Antiracist Book Club," *Vox*, November 11, 2021, vox.com/22734080/antiracist -book-club-robin-diangelo-ibram-kendi.

144 Jae Thomas, "Take Your Anti-racism Journey Further with These Online Courses," Mashable, February 24, 2021, mashable.com/deals/ anti-racism-online-courses.